MY LIFE OF RHYME

Selected Verse

Chris Month

authorHOUSE®

AuthorHouse™
1663 Liberty Drive, Suite 200
Bloomington, IN 47403
www.authorhouse.com
Phone: 1-800-839-8640

First published by AuthorHouse   4/6/2009

ISBN: 978-1-4389-6248-1 (sc)

Printed in the United States of America
Bloomington, Indiana

This book is printed on acid-free paper.

in memory of my Mother
whose foresight kept us out of the ovens
and
for Mel, my have-to-have

What is this?

This book is an anthology of poems spanning four decades. They arise from observations, reflections and imaginings. To represent reality is not the intention but rather to record what passes through the prism of the mind. Even in the instances when names are used, they serve only as fodder for satire. In a word, the poems are invention.

PART I – Longing – & PART IV – Melancholy – are an account of the feminine experience in love and related struggles. PART II – Potpourri – is a rhyming look through an ironic lens at celebrities, friends and relations and the everyday. PART III – The Tackan Years – is a compilation of occasional poems about life in an elementary school. The poems are picked from a large pool without a great deal of rhyme or reason. Though not orderly, the selection *is* representative of the entire collection.

List of Titles

PART I Longing

PART II Potpourri

PART III The Tackan Years

PART IV Melancholy

ADDENDUM

Finis

It all began a long time ago........

Mine was an extraordinary childhood. To be born Jewish in Poland in 1937 was a death sentence. To raise our chance of survival, I had to be separated from my parents. The fierceness with which I missed them was unbearable. Miraculously all three of us survived the war and we were finally reunited.

Although I was not traumatized in any obvious way, my memory of myself at that time is of a child excessively starved for attention. There was nothing I wanted more than the love and admiration of my parents and I went to great lengths to impress them. I drew pictures. I sang songs. I dressed up in my mother's skirts and high heels and put on plays. I was an actress. I was a dancer. I was a clown. But always I was an observer, studying my parents' faces for signs of approval.

One day I composed a little poem which my mother found quite moving. Full of excitement she ran to show it to my father, who being of a somewhat suspicious nature, did not believe I had written it. Assuming I had plagiarized it, he would not be convinced to the contrary unless I could prove I hadn't by composing something right then and there, in his presence. My mother became incensed at this – his lack of faith as well as his request – and a full-blown argument ensued. In no time at all I had my rhyming couplet:

> W naszym pokoju
> Niema nigdy spokoju

In English:
> In our room
> There is never any peace

There was no mistaking the admiration in my father's eyes. With six little words I had won him over. And so began my life of rhyme.

PART I Longing

The Wizard of Was

Since all the good things that I've tasted
I tasted a long time ago
And not much time's left to be wasted
It's there that I'm longing to go.

Nostalgia smiles at me, it beckons
And under its spell I must fall
I can't resist and so in seconds
I'm there and I'm heeding the call.

And all the actors in my drama
Step on the stage, come into view
A personal-patchwork-panorama
Of course, the spotlight is on you.

Though some were comic and some tragic
Each one deserves my heart's applause
But you provided what was magic
My wonderful Wizard of Was.

The Dance Lesson

Her restless eyes they moved around the dance floor
When suddenly they happened on his face
He saw her too and nothing else would matter
There just was no escaping this embrace.

He followed her outside onto the terrace
The night was ripe, the sky with stars was filled
He said, "Let's dance, I see you really want to,"
She looked into his eyes and time stood still.

She said, "You know I'm just a private dancer,
I keep my heart away from dang'rous things,"
He said, "Let go, I'll lead and you just follow,
But first stand still and let me free your wings."

He taught her steps she never knew existed
He held her tight and whirled her 'round the floor
She followed each and every move he showed her
And did turns she had never dared before.

They danced the night away in sweet abandon
The slow ones, fast ones, they did every one
And when the music stopped, a little sadness
That it was over 'ere it had begun.

She wiped the tear and thanked him for the journey
She said, "I'll see you in another life,"
He smiled and disappeared into the darkness
And she went home to be another's wife.

Wounded Women by the Roadside

At seventeen she left her home and family
In search of love, the real and lasting kind
And when she saw him she was sure she found it
But she was seventeen and love was blind.

Wounded women by the roadside
He broke their hearts and left them there
Left them crying in the darkness
Moving on without a care.
Wounded women by the roadside
He broke their hearts, he had the knack
Left them crying in the darkness
Never once did he look back.

It's true, he told her that he was a rambler
He told her that he didn't want a wife
He said he really didn't want to hurt her
But words like that mean nothing in real life.

For in his eyes she swore she saw the promise
It made no difference what his words might say
Words are not made to change the minds of dreamers
Or those who want to give their heart away.

Wounded women by the roadside
He broke their hearts and left them there
Left them crying in the darkness
Moving on without a care.
Wounded women by the roadside
He broke their hearts, he had the knack
Left them crying in the darkness
Never once did he look back.

And so he took her heart and all she offered
Which surely was the game plan from the start
And nothing about anything surprised her
Except, perhaps, the callous on her heart.

Wounded women by the roadside
He broke their hearts and left them there
Left them crying in the darkness
Moving on without a care.
Wounded women by the roadside
He broke their hearts, he had the knack
Left them crying in the darkness
Never once did he look back.

And then one day and many lovers later
She meets a man just like that other man
He says, "Don't get too close or I might hurt you,"
And she says, "Really? I sure hope you can."

Wounded women by the roadside
But she is not like all the rest
She's the one who does the leaving
She learned how from the very best.

My First Sonnet

I want to write a sonnet just for you
My first, a type I've never writ before
Though for a long time I have wanted to
    I'll try to open that poetic door.
But what should be the topic of this verse?
This specialty of Shakespeare and Millay
Should I explore, for better or for worse,
The things my heart is telling me to say?
    How every time I look into your eyes
The past comes back and washes over me,
There's something in them, and I realize
That what you see's exactly what I see.
    We keep replaying that beguine divine
That long-ago when your heart rhymed with mine.

It's Still the Same Old Story

Hello, goodbye, I'm running off, we know that that's your style
I thought that we were different, that you would stay a while
It meant a lot – too much – to me to think it might be true
But really, I was like the rest, not different, I knew.

So should I have withheld my heart and played the game like you?
Because you never spoke the words, should I have held mine too?
So I'd be able to say now, it wasn't a big deal,
You only have to learn one thing, the trick is not to feel.

I wasn't able to do that, could not forego the yen
But oh, how sad it would have been to miss what happened then.

Happy Love

There's no happy love the poets have said
They wrote and they sang and instilled in our head
That wherever there's love, it won't be there long
So I'm here to prove that the poets were wrong.

They met, fell in love and their love was divine
The feelings were mutual, no reason to pine
Their love was requited, their love it was strong
There's no doubt about it, the poets were wrong.

They dated, they married, their love grew and grew
She liked all his parts and he liked hers too
And neither one strayed, no need of a throng
So, have I convinced you the poets were wrong?

Their children were born – a girl and a boy
They were healthy and brilliant and brought only joy
They both liked their in-laws, they all got along
Do you now believe that the poets were wrong?

They always agreed – no quarrels, no fights
Not once did she long to put out his lights
And murder did not cross his mind – or divorce
The poets were wrong you're saying, of course.

And so went their life from better to best
They faced and they solved each problem and test
And she remained gorgeous and he remained strong
Need any more proof that the poets were wrong?

They both reached one hundred and death never called
She didn't get reflux, he didn't get bald
And neither one jumped from ten storeys above
The poets were wrong. There *is* happy love.

Okay, there you have it, the happy-love caper
But how pale and boring it looks down on paper
No thrill and no kill and no bite to ignite it
The poets were right in their choice not to write it.

Passion's Rise

The waters of the sea were still a while
Pushed back but now they're rising to the fore
There is confusion and disorder there
A hurricane is fast approaching shore
My heart is at high tide and tossed anew
On this risky new wave of loving you

The Opening

We went to an opening where you were a pro
You taught me so much that I didn't know
The difference between what is real and what's fake
Impressing me how not to make a mistake
The styles and techniques and colors to choose
And I listened, rapt, to the words you would use
And how I delighted in each new surprise
But all I recall is the blue of your eyes

Point of View

It's not my idea of romance
To *schlep* from one ruin to the next
The land that's so aptly called no man's
I'll pass on, I've seen enough wrecks.

Perhaps it is something I'm lacking
There *are* all those Wonders I'm told
And maybe I should be backpacking
But frankly, they just leave me cold.

A scene of which I'd be much fonder
– A corner, an alcove for two –
Just give me a sheet to get under
To ponder the wonder of you.

Eternal Flame

I won't get over you, why should I?
It would diminish what we were
And what we meant to one another
It was no momentary spur.
For once the fire was ignited
Nothing would ever be the same
At times a blaze, at times a flicker,
You, love, are my eternal flame.

If This Isn't Love

I love you's do not cross our lips
Since you don't say it, I can't
Yet, if this isn't love
This pounding for entry
This need to insume
This emptying of loins
Tell me, what is?

Blessed

We don't see each other much now
That is just the way things are
But I think about you often
And I love you from afar

And I wonder what you're doing
Who you talk to, who you see
What you're thinking, how you're feeling
If you ever think of me

And I see you there before me
In a hurry, on the run
You're seducing with a story
Or you're being charmed by one

Oft I glance you in the distance
As you're rushing down some street
Putting coins in parking meters
And it's always, oh, so sweet

Am I sad I see you less now?
No, I love you from afar
And I feel that I am blessed now
That is just the way things are

Confession

There's a dream I keep on having
That I always can recall
I'm standing somewhere very high
And I'm about to fall
It seems to be a warning
And scares me like all hell
But doesn't my subconscious know
That I already fell?

Beschert

Who knows what we are meant to be –
How much is luck, how much design?
But you were meant to be a lover,
It was my fortune you were mine.

Sunrise, Sunset

Fifty years we've been together
And you have been my life
From the children that we were when we started out
To the children that we had along the way
To the children's children now
You have done everything for me
Oh, maybe not roses on Mother's Day
Or lavish gifts
Or apartments in New York City
But when you sit next to me
As they're coming to take me to the Operating Room
And you say, I wish it could be me instead, I believe you
And I know what love is

The Heavy Dater

You had many women
You were quite a flirt
You'd take some to dinner
And some to dessert
And some to the movies
And some to a show
And then at eve's end
To her you would go
And she felt degraded
She thought it not right
But me I'd much rather
Be your last of the night

The Caller

You say you'll call later
'Cause now you can't talk
You say at 4:30
It's past 5:00 o'clock
You call at 6:30
The time's still not right
I know just what's coming
You'll call me tonight
Each time that the phone rings
I hear the same song
So what is it, honey?
The cat's got your tongue?
Each time that the phone rings
I'm nervous and tense
Will this be the moment?
I can't stand the suspense
So, darlin', have mercy
And say you'll consent
To a little less foreplay
And more main event

Slow Dance

The perfect date I dream of and desire
And one I hope someday I will still taste
Is one where all the passion and the fire
Are just a touch delayed, where there's no haste.
And while we savor the anticipation
We might break out a poem even two
We'll have a glass of wine and conversation
And tell each other tales long overdue.
And we will kiss but slowly, softly, sweetly
Desire will light our movie's every frame
We won't give in until lit up completely
I like this teasing aspect of the game.
But it won't be today – I'm out of luck
You take one look at me and say, "Let's…"

Insistence

I never saw it as insistence
Just an exchange between two friends
Maybe subconsciously it's distance
You want and I can understand
Unrealistic is my vision
Of how exactly we should be
I should have learned from each collision
But some things I don't want to see.

Familiarity breeds contempt
And even lovers aren't exempt.

Reunion

A name from the past, he starts to remember
A girl from that time, that time long ago
Fifty years gone, it's almost a lifetime
Does she remember? He's dying to know.

A voice from the past, she starts to remember
A boy from that time, a boy she once knew
How did they meet? Does he remember?
What did they talk about? What did they do?

A glimpse of the past, and yes, she remembers
And what she recalls is they had a romance
Is she correct? She needs him to tell her
And time's getting short. This might be their last chance.

Fast Forward

I read your note, the song begins
It's hot and I hear violins
And we are there, it's skin to skin,
Can one atone before the sin?

The Red Dress

It was the time of the red dress
I knew your favorite was red
And I was lost in happiness
"Like Carmen," I think's what you said

A night in winter, blizzard, snow
I took no weatherman's advice
I had to meet you, had to go
But I was driving on thin ice

No danger would have stopped me then
Not ice below nor snow above
They held no candle to my yen
I had to answer, called by love

A flushed face in the glass I see
The hungry eyes, the loosened hair
The ribbon which has set it free
And the red dress thrown o'er a chair

That dress hangs in my closet still
But unlike me, as good as new
And every detail, every frill
Reminds me of that night with you

Refrain

A boy barely twenty
With green eyes and black hair
And a poetic line
So, of course, she is there.

The girl, a dark beauty
With a sexy derriere
And cleavage to match
And, oh yes, he is there.

They look and they touch
There are sparks in the air
And the whole world is young
It is called an affair.

Many forks in the road
Leading oft' to despair
But when they converge
There is something still there.

And just when we think
We've got time left to spare
There's a voice in the night
Warning us, "Au contraire."

Yes, our bodies will break
Break beyond all repair
But love will survive
Love will always be there.

That Tear

At one time your insults cut to the core
They serve now to prove I don't care anymore
Where once you could hurt me and cause me great pain
Those times are gone, they will not come again
You no longer bring that tear to my eye
And I, who once did, do not want to die

The Cure

There was a time when I was sick with love
A feeling I just couldn't rise above
My body ached, my fever rose sky high
I didn't know if I would live or die
The doctors could do nothing for my pain
They said that broken hearts weren't their domain
They had no pills, no knowledge to impart
Could do no magic by-pass of my heart.

I knew I was alone and when no help arrived
I cured myself of you and I survived.

Twisted

No, you can't hurt me anymore
For I'm done crying at your door
You know those crumbs that you would throw?
That craving ended long ago

And you no longer cause me pain
So all your trying is in vain
For I will not again be burned
At least not where *you* are concerned

No, you can't hurt me, lost your spell
And this I know and know it well
That I am cured, and I won't call
But, oh, how much I miss it all

Distraction

That your distraction's due to me
You've hinted from the very start
I'm flattered, but I won't be blamed
For your unconquerable heart

Roots or Wings

You say tomato and I say *tomahto*
You say potato and I say *potahto*
But you say when the good times are all gone
It's time for moving on
And I say for better or for worse.

How does it end, how does it end
– The singer wonders as he sings –
When one wants roots, the other wings?

If

I see you standing there once more
And think of all those times before
And wonder if it still could be
If we were free, if we were free…

The warmth of flesh, the scent of skin
The invitation to come in
Could we repeat what was sublime?
Had we but time, had we but time…

There'd be no need for wondering this
These doubts we'd easily dismiss
And reach for those notes still unsung
If we were young, if we were young…

Love in the Time of Anthrax

(To the tune of *Here Is My Heart*)

Ignoring the bombs and the anthrax
Tall buildings, the sound of alarms
Planes flying low, trains and tunnels
I know I'll be safe in your arms.
On a day like today when I'm meeting you
There's fear in my heart but there's happiness too-oo.

Now that we're here, let me hold you
Missed you so, did you know?
And all of the things that I told you
Long ago, they're still so
Now that we're here, now that we're here.

It's hard to find pleasure in living
With all that we're being put through
But that doesn't stop me from dreaming
That maybe I'll find some with you.
On a day like today when I'm meeting you
There's fear in my heart but there's happiness too-oo.

Now that you're here let me hold you
Missed you so, did you know?
And all of the things that I told you
Long ago, they're still so
Now that we're here, now that we're here.

We have traveled from afar
Here I am and here you are
For a moment let us stay
Let's stay together
Just a moment's all we have
Close your eyes and let's make love
Who knows when we'll meet again?
Who knows if ever?

Now that we're here let me hold you
Missed you so, did you know?
And all of the things that I told you
Long ago, they're still so
Now that we're here, now that we're here.

It's Just Impossible to Comprehend
(Villanelle)

How very quickly everything can end,
One moment here and the next here no more,
It's just impossible to comprehend.

No time to say goodbye, to make amends,
And never to find out what lay in store,
How very quickly everything can end.

An airplane just beginning to ascend,
While some rush to the Tower's topmost floor,
It's just impossible to comprehend

That Destiny'd be waiting round the bend
To wed them and so cruelly underscore
How very quickly everything can end.

Plane hits the Tower, a ball of fire, the end,
And nothing will again be as before,
It's just impossible to comprehend.

But memory ends too and so I've penned
These thoughts as a reminder evermore
How very quickly everything can end,
It's just impossible to comprehend.

PART II Potpourri

Life of a Ladies' Man

Well, you're Leonard, you're our poet
You have traveled near and far
Singing love songs, making music
It's just you and your guitar
But of course there are the women
Can't resist you, you're their man
There is Joan and Jane and Nancy
And oh, yes, there's Marianne

And you take them to the river
And on mountains high above
There are chocolates in their boxes
And there ain't no cure for love
And you love them and you leave them
Yes, you leave them all behind
All those legions of admirers
Of your body and your mind

There's Suzanne and Lady Midnight
Who of love say they will die
But you know all about partings
You know how to say goodbye
And you want them in Vienna
And you want them in Japan
And you offer them a waltz and
Yes, you're everybody's man.

But we know that soon you'll tire
Everything becomes old hat
So you go up on Mount Baldy
With those monks, so what's with that?
And we're glad you're finally off there
Why'd you leave? We'll take a shot –
You can live without religion
Without women, you cannot.

Quoth the Maven

Once upon an evening dreary,
I was sitting weak and weary
Reading *Newsday* in the hope of
Relaxation, nothing more.
Saw a poem by Vitello
Which just wasn't very mellow
And which made me very angry,
Anger I had to explore.
Why this anger you might ask me,
Anger to my very core?
Paul says teachers are a bore!

I read on with trepidation
This attack on education
And I knew deep down inside
I'd have to even up the score.
'Twas a cinch 'cause Paul's no maven
On the poem called, *The Raven*,
If he were, then he would know
That scansion poets can't ignore,
That a poet with no scansion
Is a poet we deplore,
Only this and nothing more.

And I bet my bottom dollar
That when Paul was still a scholar
Learning poetry mechanics
He considered it a bore.
So perhaps that's why Vitello
Is no Shakespeare or Longfellow
He may be a fine reporter
But his poems do not soar,
And his name does not appear
In books that house poetic lore,
Not today and nevermore.

All Shook Up

You weren't in a hound dog mood
The talk was going very well
And even though your phone gave out
Nobody sang *Heartbreak Hotel*.

We talked about *Venus* that morn
The film that stars Peter O'Toole
I told you what it was about,
Forgot to say, "Please don't be cruel."

What it's about is an old man
Who's frail and sick but one who still
Has longings, fantasies, desires,
Ones that he knows he can't fulfill.

You said, "Did you identify?"
As you stepped on my suede shoes blue
But still I chose not to reply,
Did not say what I wanted to.

A Song for Bob

Well, you're my performing artist
And I love all of your tricks
Me I've got to serve somebody
That is how I get my kicks
Once a girl of the North Country
I was tangled up in blue
And if now this wheel's on fire
'Twould not be if not for you.

I remember how it started
Heading south on a slow train
I got stuck inside of Mobile
With those Memphis blues again
And the times they were-a-changing
And your eyes were like the dawn
And, of course, just like a woman
I was going, going, gone.

In my boots of Spanish leather
I'd come watch the river flow
And then when your ship would come in
I just couldn't let you go
All I'd really want to do is
Linger there and take your cures
Spanish is the loving tongue
But it does not compare to yours.

One more night, restless farewell
And you go your way, I go mine
But I want you, yes, I want you
And tomorrow's a long time
And it's true time passes slowly
Oh, to be alone with you
But there'll be another night 'cause
It's not over baby blue.

The Best Song I Never Heard

(To the tune of *I'm Not There*)

A song becomes a movie which could just be common fare
But when the singer's Dylan and the song is *I'm Not There*
And when the grapevine has it – and the grapevine's never wrong –
That *I'm Not There* is definitely Dylan's greatest song
– Paul Williams and Greil Marcus and John Bauldie say that it
Is not just Dylan's greatest but the greatest ever writ –
Well, I of course must hear it and no effort will be spared
Until I find that wonder, find that song called *I'm Not There*.

And yes, I do, I find it and it's here in front of me
And I can't wait to play it on this *Basement Tapes* CD
I put it on the player, the earphone in my ear
And…huh… what's this, this mumbling? For mumbling's what I
hear.
Just what is our Bob saying? It is something 'bout *a veil*
But then again it could be that he's really saying *tail*
Or maybe it is *weight* he's saying, maybe it is *way*
Or maybe *while*, or *wheel*, or *wail* or could it be… *oy vey*?

Those legendary words of yore, words mythical and fabled
They're gone, instead just mumblings, so…is Bob learning disabled?
And this goes on five minutes more, can't understand a word
This could be Dylan's greatest song, best song I never heard.

Tom Waits & Company

Of all the singers that I knew
The best I liked Tom Waits
And so I called him up one day
And asked him if he dates
He said, *why not*, but I was late
And he had had to run
And that is when I realized
That Tom Waits for no ONE

Timon of Athens

Of all the Greeks that I once knew
I liked that Timon best
He came from Athens, that I know
But I don't know the rest
And so I called him up one day
But he had had to run
And that is when I realized
Timon waits for no ONE

The Dime

Of all the banks that I have known
I liked The Dime the best
And so I called them up one day
And said I would invest
They said, *come in*, but I was late
And they had had to run
And that is when I realized
The Dime waits for no ONE

Haym

Of all the names that I have liked
I always liked Haym best
And when I learned he was Tom's dad
I was still more impressed
I said, *let's meet*, but I was late
And he had had to run
And that is when I realized
That Haym waits for no ONE

Tom (Still) Waits

The lobby's full of folks today
There's Bill and Bob, the Mormon
There's Miss Demeanor and Miss Deed
Tom Waits, now a longshoreman
They're waiting here while I call up
It's hard to be a doorman
Still I ring Mr. Mailer's flat
And say, *Tom Waits for Norman*

Take Me Out to the Ballgame

I'm sick of the movies they're making these days
They're not sexy, romantic or clever
They bore me to tears, I can hardly stay up
During each directorial endeavor.

When I saw *Dying Young*, I thought, not young enough
Jungle Fever was no less a pain
I could show that Spike Lee how to do the right thing –
By not making a movie again.

And who's Kevin Costner and what does he want?
Why the heck won't he leave us alone?
Is he lacking for partners and so dances with wolves?
To the wolves he should have been thrown.

Perhaps what we need is a bonfire or two
How to fuel them could be a pleasure
We'd start with the *Vanities*, add *Godfather III*
And Mike Nichols throw in for good measure.

Well, I'm getting angry so I'd better stop
These violent thoughts will not do
But ere I withdraw, just a word about *Alice*
I would terminate her too.

Dear Mr. Marlowe

Come live with you and be your love
Is something that I cannot do
Maybe I could have way back then
But not in 1992.

How can we sit upon the rocks
And watch the shepherds feed their flocks
When all the rocks are full of grime
And all the shepherds doing time?

How can you make me beds of roses
When underneath our very noses
The garbage piles block out the sky
And all around the homeless lie?

As for that gown of finest wool
Which from our pretty lambs we'd pull –
There are no lambs, they've been polluted
And gowns are all reconstituted.

Those fur-lined slippers for the cold
With buckles of the finest gold –
Come on! Get real! Not on the street!
The muggers would cut off my feet!

So, as you see, our world is such
That lambs and sheep won't get you much
But don't despair, I'm not above
A little bit of toxic love.

Dear Mr. Hardy

Higgledy, Piggledy
Tess of the D'Urbervilles
Roman Polanski has
Shown me that you're
Easier to grasp via
Cinematography
You've become clearer while
Jude's still obscure

Dear Mr. Proust

Marcel Proust was a writer who'll last
His *Remembrance* will ne'er be outclassed
I know I'm no equal
But I'm writing a sequel
Called *Forgetfulness of Things Past*

Oh, Mr. Sartre

The secret has finally been writ
Why in bed Jean Paul Sartre was a hit
So how did he do it?
There's nothingness to it.
Seduction and cuddling, that's it.

Oh, Dr. Freud...

The scholars have finally spoke
His sister-in-law Freud did poke
It seems in the case
Of Minna Bernays
A cigar was not just a smoke.

The New Math

John Kennedy had legions
Abe Lincoln had four score
And Valentino, Casanova
Sade had even more
Bill Clinton is still counting
His figure's pretty high
And Jeffrey Mason says 2K
But he's been known to lie.

And now *you're* quoting numbers
Of ladies' hearts you've won
So did you hump more broads than even
Donalds Trump and Juan?

Dear Mr. Tiger

You ask me why campfires I seek
I have a primordial streak
My brain's such a mystery
It remembers prehistory
But not what transpired last week

Dear Andrea Marcovicci

Dear Andrea Marcovicci, your new record is your best
But the song called *Do You Miss Me?* really puts you to the test
Though the lyric's very clever, there is one spot that is sore
See, it's not I'm happy *like*, but *as* I've never been before,
Because *like*'s a preposition which is used before a phrase
Whereas *as* is a conjunction – have I got you in a daze?
And *I've never been before*, is not a phrase, it is a clause
And a clause needs a conjunction. Those are English grammar laws.

Have Pity, Mr. Simon

John Simon picks up paper and pen
To praise the "extreme simplicity" of Verlaine.
I don't know who his muse is
But here are some of the words he uses:
Verbosity, prolixity, finitude, archizing
Quasi-molossus, pleonastic (twice), *quadrisyllabic-izing*
Denudedness, ellipsis, dilettantism, climactic
Anathema, attitudinizing, recherché, didactic.

Mister Simon, does anyone really talk like this?
I'm adding *pompous blowhard* to the list.

All the Writing Skills are Gone
(To the tune of *Where have all the Flowers Gone?*)

All the writing skills are gone
No one can write
Secretaries, principals
Writing's a blight.

Sentences do not exist
Where have they gone?
If they do, they're pages long
They're all run-on.

Verb and noun agreement's lost
Yes, times are lean
Tenses changing in mid-thought
What does it mean?

Apostrophes have gone away
Adverbs for sure
And good spelling is passé
Spell check's no cure.

Grammar's hit-or-miss these days
And rarely taught
Rules are bad for self-esteem
Mistakes are not.

Teacher's Lament
(To the tune of *Trading Up*)

I'm sitting on the train and people are talking
Talking so loud they could wake the dead
And almost every word those people are saying
Is incorrect and makes me see red.

It's, *between you and I* and *between he and she*
And I really want to object
But I keep my mouth shut and I don't say a word
So, their grammar is incorrect.

And it's, *I'm like* and *he's like* and *we're like* and *they're like*
And I really want to object
But I keep my mouth shut and I don't say a word
So, their grammar is incorrect.

I don't know how much more of this I can take
I find myself holding my breath
But when, *she axed him this* and *he axed her that*
I finally axed them to death.

An Ax to Grind

Let me be blunt with you, you say
And I don't want to carp
But when you're being blunt with me
Aren't you really being sharp?

The Empty Basement Blues
(To the tune of *Learning the Blues*, sort of)

The basement is empty, like never before
The mess is all gone now, I can walk on the floor
The books and the papers and magazines tossed
The basement is empty and I'm feeling lost.

I remember the times I'd walk down those stairs
And spend hours looking for something down there
But in time, eventually, even I knew
That, yes, a cleanup was long overdue.

So we threw out the records, those 50's LP's
They were dusty and moldy and carried disease
The crib from the 60's, we threw that out too
The basement is empty and I'm feeling blue.

Somehow I remember that basement with pleasure
The times I went down there and returned with a treasure
The basement is empty, a bare I can't bear
'Cause I know now I'll never find anything there.

An Examination of Sorts

A life unexamined is worthless
So claims Plato's still famous line
And Plato was one smart Greek cookie
That's why I'm examining mine

But where should I start to examine?
Let's see, how about in this drawer?
Some letters from beaus from the '50s
A Playbill from May '64

A matchbook marked Café Allegro
A postcard from some town in Spain
A snapshot of two forms in shadow
Who took it that summer in Maine?

A pink satin rose, a lace ribbon
Pressed leaves wearing colors of fall
A photo of some handsome stranger
Whose name I no longer recall

Some trinkets from seaside locations
Where several vacations I spent
A shell from the Cape where I summered
A letter addressed but not sent

Or maybe I'll start in this closet
Examine the clothes that here lie
The minis, the maxis, the midis
The styles of those days long gone by

The sandals I wore when I met you
The ribbon that held up my hair
The dress I put on for that meeting
But only to take it off there

This house where so long I've resided
With all my existence is rife
I look and I think and remember
And thus I examine my life

So then, is my life now worth living?
And would what I did Plato please?
Or is what I've done nothing more than
Just sift through my fond memories?

Not Virtue or Evil or Duty
And less like Greek drama than soap
So should I be grateful to Plato?
Or maybe I'll just thank Bob Hope.

So Much to Know

My dryer has asbestos
My fish has mercury
My sweeteners have cyclamates
And smoking's bad for me

My bacon has nitrates
My butter has fat
My hair dye has something
That just killed a rat

My Darvon's addictive
My water's impure
My air's radioactive
Tomorrow for sure

My subways have muggers
Who all mean me harm
My pumps have no gas'line
All headlines alarm

Oh, give me back the fifties
When I didn't know all this
When life was, oh, so boring
And ignorance was bliss.

On Forgetting

I must accept it's getting worse
This memory loss is such a curse
Once I was quick, now I am dense
And there's no help from supplements
All vitamins I had to ditch
After forgetting which was which
Ginko Biloba I forsook
Could not remember what I took
For memory loss there is no cure
It's something that I must endure.

But every evening when I see
The nightly news on my TV
And watch the pols parading by
And listen as they testify
I'm quite amazed, for who'd have guessed
That they remember even less.

The Mind's Eye

One time she was a beauty
And oh, he told her so
His eyes, his words approving
So many moons ago

The years have done their damage
His passion's not been quelled
She's no longer that beauty
He doesn't see that well

Huh?

We know that forgetting can be quite upsetting
And there isn't a thing can be done
It does not take a sage to tell us that age
Will take pris'ners and mem'ry is one
And so I accept it, I even expect it
I will not remember, and yet –
How come I recall every detail, yes all
Of the things that I'd *like* to forget?

The Relentless Decades

Ten's an adventure
Twenty a lark
Thirty desire
Forty a spark
Fifty a song that
Sixty still sings
But seventy, seventy
Oh, seventy stings

Summer of '08

The news is bad from all around
There is no happy day
Some little jerk who rules Iran
Wants to blow us away.

Gas prices have gone through the roof
While stock prices are down
Contaminated food supply
The pols have all left town.

The terrorists are at our door
They can't wait to attack
And who'll be there to guard us all?
Oh, no! Might be Barack!

Republicans and Democrats
All hate each others' guts
The only question seems to be
Which party is more nuts?

Oh, take me back to days of yore
When all that caused distress
Was whether *is* is really *is*
And Monica's blue dress.

A-Hailin' Sarah Palin

(To the tune of *The Times they are A-Changin'*)

They're gathering 'round wherever you roam
They're all lining up set to cast the first stone
They'd like nothing more than to break all your bones
They're good, oh, so good at assailin'
Because you're a woman and beautiful too
How they hate you, Sarah Palin.

They hack and they smear as they're looking for smut
Your son is a druggie, your daughter a slut
And having five kids means you must be a nut
How they hope that soon you'll be failin'
Because you're a woman and beautiful too
How they hate you, Sarah Palin.

They trash and insult you and use every tack
To injure, offend, to demean and attack
They'll stab you in front and they'll stab you in back
Oh, they're good, they're good at derailin'
Because you're a woman and beautiful too
How they hate you, Sarah Palin.

But the strength you display in the face of these lies
Just shows you much smarter, much abler, more wise
And so while they gleefully plan your demise
You're out there and you are prevailin'
They're jealous and envious 'cause you have it all
So they hate you, Sarah Palin.

Now whether you make it to VP or not
You've already made it, there's no one more hot
Unlike all those libbies who'll soon be forgot
It's you that the crowds are all hailin'
Pelosi and Boxer and Steinem and Dowd
They don't get you, Sarah Palin.

The Regulars and the Elites

When I was young the thing to be
Was to be different – that was me
And so elite I was back then
But I no longer have that yen
Now everyone's elite, they are
And so I'm glad I'm reg-u-LAR

Reason and Feeling

The talk now turns to politics
The candidates, the dirty tricks
We obviously do not agree
In this debate we should not be.

I think you think that I'm deranged
You can't believe how much I've changed
How much I've changed? I disagree
Maybe I'm finally being me.

Getting Along

We can't talk about politics
At all my views you scoff
We can't talk 'bout the things I do
You think that's showing off

My stories mostly leave you cold
They either tire or bore
And we can't talk about the past
That topic you abhor

The justice system is off bounds
We sing a different tune
And if I disagree with you
My morals you impugn

We can't talk about Art or Lit
My tastes there you disdain
You say I only see the trees
The forest's your domain.

It's obvious that we don't talk much
As from this you can tell
And maybe that's the reason why
We get along so well.

To Talk or Not To Talk

To talk about religion, you said it wasn't nice
For politics and money you gave the same advice
But what I am proposing is, next time please insist
We also add Diseases to that dreaded not-nice list.

Vacance à Quatre

We found this lovely spot in Huberdeau
Auberge la loutre where twice now we did go
Pure mountain air, a lake shimmering clear
The stillness is the only thing you hear.

We go with brother Gerry and wife Lin
The *pièce de résistance* is the cuisine
A lovely dining room has this hotel
We eat to strains of Georges Brassens, Jacques Brel
Three hour dinners every single night
With Floyd who smartly serves up each delight.

The repartee is fun and good the mood
We do not talk of Bush or war, just food
The menu is in French but that's okay
'Cause Floyd explains each *terrine*, each *pâté*
Canard magret? Lin says it's something fat
So none of us is gonna order that
Then while we're eating, by this thought we're struck
That we were all too chicken to get duck.

The running joke at breakfast every day
Is how in French this phrase to *prononcer*
Œuf à la coque and just what does it mean
And is it cock or coke or something in between?
And someone wants to know what is the rule
I wouldn't touch it with a ten foot *poule*.

Then for our coffee, Floyd brings the milk *chaud*
That's how it should be served and Floyd should know
His mother comes from Venice. Lin says, "Oh?
My mother served it cold in Buffalo."

And when Lin has the floor we're sure to hear
All about animals, her love most dear
But thanks to Lin I'm no longer alarmed
She tells me animals mean me no harm
All animals are innocent she'll deem
Humans she doesn't hold in such esteem
And then, what is outlandish ev'n for her
She says she knows a dog who can say *hamburger*.
"Can he say *fries*?" I wonder but don't say.
The twilight zone cannot be far away.
And Lin cannot sit still, won't take a break
She's either in the kayak or the lake
Or in the paddleboat or on a bike
There isn't anything she doesn't like
The Dollar stores are also on her plate
And, oh, one other thing, she's always late
Though I can't figure out why this should be
Because there's no one drives as fast as she.

And Gerry's ever sporting a good mood
He has that wonderful Month attitude
He's friendly to our waiter, loves to chat
But Floyd does not speak Yiddish and that's that
And so he cannot order in that tongue
But we all know that Gerry can't go wrong,
Whatever language he may order in
He'll end up eating *la même chose* as Lin.

Then there is Mel who also loves the floor
He's a contender from the days of yore
But often when he talks, our minds will roam
For he can talk until the cows come home
And every topic is his specialty
What he loves best is when we don't agree
Of course, we know his thinking's very deep
That's why it puts us into a deep sleep
And if not with the brilliance of his talks
He tortures us with all those five mile walks
Still, everything he does must be just so
Because he's *anal* he will have you know
But that is horse manure is what I say
I think that Mel just wants to have his way.

Well, now I'm done my ragging of those three
I s'ppose that I should turn the pen on me
On second thought, I think that I'll refrain
And let a little mystery remain.

And so good bye to all we found so dear –
The food, the lake, the mountains – till next year.

Paradise Lost

Well, I'm off to St. Croix, that paradise island
I'll lie on the beaches of the Caribbean Sea
I'll swim in its waters so green and so limpid
There's no one as lucky as me!

I'll fly eight miles high over mountains and oceans
American, Pan Am, Swissair and what not
I'll touch down in Paris and drive to Geneva
There's no one who's got what I've got.

I'll eat escargots and shop chez Dior and
I'll meet the most daring and fabulous men
I'll take lots of pictures of all the right ruins
I won't want to go home again.

Well, it rained in Paree and it poured in Geneva
And it thundered and lightened on Paradise Isle
My luggage was lost, my pictures are rotten
And the dress that I bought's out of style.

The food gave me ptomaine, the planes gave me jet lag
I got such a headache I thought I would die
And as for the men that were gonna be daring
The guy next to me's scared to fly.

So do not say Paris, do not say Vienna
Or Zurich or Tokyo or Athens or Rome
I'd more than my share of exotic places
Next summer you'll find me at home.

Spare Me

I don't want to know what the altitude is
That word itself makes me ill
Just fly the damn plane
To the place where I'm bound
I've already taken two pills

Don't inform me the weather is sunny and good
Or worse yet, it's foggy and dull
Just fly the darn plane
To the place I get off
Before I go out of my skull

I couldn't care less if we're passing the Falls
Your appeals to me are in vain
But if somehow you could
Kind of fly straight and smooth
I might still come out of this sane

I need not be shown all the beautiful sights
Just your voice on that *thing* is a pain
By the way, while you're leisurely
Chatting with me
Who the heck is flying this plane?

The guy on my left is making a film
The one on my right's getting smashed
And me – every sound and
Sensation I feel
Assures me we're going to crash

So who needs your voice on that object of doom?
By now I know every line
If you have a problem
Don't tell it to me
And I promise, I won't tell you mine.

Chris Takes the Bus

(To the tune of *The Twelve Days of Christmas*)

On the bus to Montreal
There were lots of things to see
10 Puerto Ricans
9 Guys with earrings
8 No speak English
7 Booming boxes
6 Would be killers
Not counting the driver
And a white, single, paranoid, ME!

Aprime El Numero Dos

I bought a new hair dryer
Didn't know 'twould pose a threat
It comes with many warnings
More than for a gun, I bet.
The danger overwhelms me
I break out in a sweat
No help from the directions
Not a word of English yet.

Most Wanted

Today I committed a most heinous crime
For which I am sure I'll be doing time
The place was King Kullen, the checkout Express
And I had *twelve* items which is not ten or less

The cashier looked down at me with disdain
I could see that my crime was causing her pain
Those two extra items near drove her berserk
I knew not the pride she took in her work

So quick I got out, that girl was no fun
And she had my number in more ways than one
Those two extra items would give her no peace
Soon I'll be arrested by the checkout police

Bon Appétit

I'm eating much more than I oughta
Some foods I just cannot resist
Has anyone seen my waist somewhere?
I think that it does not exist

The way of all flesh is upon me
The weight of the world is there too
I'll have to do something about it
Like starting to diet anew

I throw out all chocolate and candy
Get rid of each earthly delight
And banish all ice cream and cookies
I will not take even one bite

I diet and diet and diet
It's Atkins and Stillman and such
My clothes are soon going to fit me
I don't have to lose all that much

I weigh myself once every hour
I do this each day without fail
I'm fed up with what the scale shows me
I'll just have to get a new scale!

Hair Today

She calls because she has lots to report
She cut her hair today, it's really short
It doesn't look so good, her face looks fat
And she goes on and on and on like that.

She used to wear it that way when a girl
But then it wasn't straight, it used to curl
Perhaps she ought to dye it blond instead
Perhaps she doesn't know I'm seeing red.

I guess she doesn't know and doesn't care
That I am getting bored with all that hair
And it gets on my nerves that she can't see
I want to talk 'bout deeper things – like me.

The Empty Nest
(Sometime before they left)

We who are mothers have long been impressed
To dread the coming of the empty nest
The day's bound to dawn and it's 'round the bend
When the kids will leave and our life will end
Guess I'm different 'cause would you believe
That the thing I dread is that they won't leave?

A Keen Tot

When I was young and pretty
There was so much to admire
My hair was black and shiny
My lips were red as fire
My skin was smooth and silky
My eyes green as the sea
I had a million boy friends
Who wished to marry me
They liked my face and figure
My each and every part
My hips and thighs and waistline
They offered me their heart.

But those years are long gone now
Their damage done, I fear
And where are those admirers
– The ones of yesteryear –
Who said my eyes were diamonds
Who said my lips were rubies?
Now, only tot Eliza
Is keen to see my boobies.

My Gynecologist

My female gynecologist
Is down to earth, not phony
She seems to shoot straight from the hip
No bullshit or baloney.
And so, on my last visit there
I quite intended to
Inquire about estrogen
And ask what *she* would do.
Would she prescribe it for a friend?
Her daughter or her mother?
But very soon I realized
I wouldn't have to bother.
I wouldn't have to pose those words,
"Good? Bad? Pray tell which is it?"
Because she kept fanning herself
Through my entire visit.

The Mammogram

I had my mammogram today
The day that I love best
The nurse, she poked and pinched and squeezed
Attacking each poor breast
She posed me every way there is
Ten times, I was getting weak
What was it she was shooting there?
The movie of the week?
And then the X-rays spewed forth
Real great *that* made me feel!
And worst, the radiologist
Behind that wall of steel –
The man who holds life in his hands
With mystery's imbued
Just like an executioner
Under his cape and hood.

So now I'm waiting, seems like hours
Why does it take so long?
Of course, I know, that's what it is,
There must be something wrong!
Yes, this is it, the end is near
So much for long life-spans
And while I sit half-naked there
I make my funeral plans.
And then the door, it opens wide
She's back, I hope good news
That's when I hear my fav'rite words,
"We need a few more views."

My Busy Life
(To the tune of *Christmas in Kilarney*)

The mammogram, the breast exam
At doctors and surgeons is where I am
It's Christmas in Kilarney
It's Doctorsville here at home.

The estrogen, the sweats again
The visits to my OBGYN
It's Christmas in Kilarney
It's Doctorsville here at home.

The door is always open
My doctor's always in
And he and I are practicing
Preventive medicine.

So I invest in every test
Bone density, Pap smear and all the rest
It's Christmas in Kilarney
It's Doctorsville here at home.

The thing that's so amazing
The thing that doesn't click
Is why I go through all this woe
When I'm not even sick.

I guess I see, it has to be
'Cause I've reached the age of maturity
I can't go to Kilarney
Unless all my Docs go too.

Next?

They told us the benefits would be immense
Our hearts would be strong, our bones would be dense
Our skin and our hair would start in to mend
Depression would lift, the hot flashes end
They promised long life and fracture-free hips
And we, of course, listened to their godlike lips.

But now there is trouble in Estrogen Land
Some lousy statistics on which no one planned
And now that we're being left in the lurch
They're going to hide behind their research
And blame one another, the final debasement
While we, we all die of hormone replacement.

Therapy

Bipolar, bulimic or phobic
Or lacking desire and zeal
Compulsive-obsessive or manic-depressive
A label for each way we feel.

Professional help is the answer
By talking it out we'll reveal
Just what there is hid in our ego and id
That makes us behave like a heel.

For me it is not the right answer
I won't be consulting a shrink
Because if I knew why I do what I do
I'd feel much more rotten, I think.

Hell... O-Oh!

Twenty Common Phobias, Netscape is advertising
The fact that I have most of them is not a bit surprising
There's fear of flying, spiders, snakes, of crowds, diseases, heights
Of open spaces, fire, water, earthquakes, stings and bites
And then I come to the last one, and well, what do you know?
There seems to be a fear of death – I wanna say Hell... O-Oh!

The Face Lift

It's the year of the wrinkle, the year of the creases
My face looks like hell, my panic increases
Remedies beckon, so many I see
Online and in ads and, of course, on TV.
There's collagen, botox, they'll give me a shot
And, no, they don't tell each with danger is fraught
They promise I'll look like J.Lo – that sends shivers
(I'm dying to ask what they did to Joan Rivers.)
So should I succumb to this lifting of faces
Or simply stay out of all well lit places?

The Fountain of Youth

In this age of strong alliance
'Tween Technology and Science
Even psychics, even sages
Can't tell what a person's age is
For we now have weight reduction
Creams and pills and liposuction
Lines have disappeared from skin
Cosmetic surgery is in
Everybody has been shifted
Nipped and tucked and raised and lifted
No one's bald and no one's graying
For there's dyeing and toupéing
Everybody looks so sporty –
Are they sixty? Are they forty?
Are they more or are they less?
It's impossible to guess.
So I have set myself a task
And I observe, I do not ask
My method works, it's quite terrific
– Okay, so it's not scientific –
But I'm becoming quite a whiz
And my conclusion? Here it is:
Watch how they get out of a car
After they've traveled near or far
The younger ones they simply beat it
The oldies can't get up once seated.

The Retirement Disease

A silent prayer: Please, oh, please
Let us then not talk of disease.

I do not need to learn about
Poor Mary's stroke or Harry's gout
If you don't mind, I'd rather not
Discuss the size of Nina's clot
And keep from me all information
Of everybody's medication
Do not report chapter and verse
Of anyone who's getting worse
Who cannot walk, who cannot think
Who cannot hear, who cannot blink
Who's lacking tone and losing bone
And can no longer live alone.

Yes, put on hold this talk incessant
At least till I've had my anti-depressant!

Welcome to the Fabulous Fifties

There are those who think
That life starts at fifty
It really doesn't, it ends
So this birthday party
Adds insult to injury
Are you sure these people are friends?

'Cause friends are supposed to
Be honest and level
Speak truthfully, don't you agree?
So I will be honest
And tell you the truth, dear
I'll tell you the way things will be:

You won't write that novel
Or marry Paul Newman
Or tap dance on some Broadway stage
But you will get worse headaches
You will get worse backaches
'Cause nothing gets better with age

You won't conquer Wall Street
Play Scarlett O'Hara
Discover that long sought for cure
You'll start counting wrinkles
You'll start counting phobias
Oh, that you can count on for sure

You won't climb Mount Everest
Or star in an Art film
Or live in the White House with Bill
You will start to droop, though
Your hair will turn silver
From now on all things are downhill

You won't be Mick Jagger
You won't be Madonna
You won't be Picasso or Freud
You will be near-sighted
You will be stooped over
And probably soon unemployed

You won't win the Downhill
You won't win the Preakness
You won't win the Great Books debate
You will lose your glasses
You will lose your car keys
The one thing you won't lose is weight!

You won't meet the Bushes
Obamas won't visit
And Hillary won't make a fuss
The Pope is too busy
O.J.'s still on trial
You're stuck with real big shots like us.

What I have predicted
It's all gonna happen
But that is no cause for despair
Because it gets better
Oh yes, it gets better
By sixty you won't even care!

Mother's Day

Three hundred sixty-four days of the year
They show us no interest at all
Unless they need something, then have no fear
They're sure to give us a call

Our all grownup children have lives of their own
For that is the way of life's game
And I am not here their acts to condone
Or, for that matter, to blame

The truth is, I like that they've lives of their own
And I hope that's the way it will stay
My only objection, and I'm not alone
Is that second Sunday in May:

The roadways are jammed, the restaurants packed
There isn't a place I can go
As they try to make up what the whole year they lacked
With a vengeance that only kids know.

Of all those prepackaged Days I abhor
'Twould seem Mother's Day I least prize
So why, when that plant arrives at the door
Am I standing there wiping my eyes?

Girlfriends

Like long lost lovers parched for contact
Across the miles we try to touch
Writing our life in daily doses
E-mail has never meant so much

What is it that so fascinates us
And holds our interest for so long?
The need to know, to ask, to tell all
Who would have thought 'twould be so strong?

Our friendship forged in adolescence
Lay dormant all these years, who knew
That just an E-mail'd reawaken
Girlfriends from 1952?

Dancing Queen

The Kings they have their Queens
The pearls they have the seas
And Liz she has her Dick
But we have you, Louise.

And Lancelot had Guenevere
The birds they have the trees
And Liz, she also had her Nick
But we have you, Louise.

And Romeo had Juliet
The beach it has its breeze
And Liz had Eddie, Michaels, John
But we have you, Louise.

So we dance our little hearts out
Yes, each and every one
Dancing With the Stars
Was never as much fun!

The French Are Not Like Us

The French are so well adjusted
The affairs, the "amants", the "maitresses"
They hop from one bed to another
With never a moment of stress
They do not feel jealous or guilty
They're certainly not insecure
They're always so honest with spouses
So civilized and so mature.
But if everything's so hunky-dory
And "l'amour toujours" is so great
How come the French hold the record
For the highest suicide rate?

The Ears Have It

A fortieth birthday can be mighty depressing
But the right kind of jewel makes it less so, we're guessing
The earrings arrived, a diamond expression
And four-point-one karats can lift a depression.

The joy it was boundless, the thank-you's enormous
That man is the best, they would proudly inform us
And we who had nothing to do with the show
Felt the magic of diamonds. We basked in their glow.

Aware that the way to a man's heart was through
His stomach, we were; but now we know too
– And this to you wooers we'd like to convey –
That the way to a woman's is through Cartier.

A Hallmark Moment

Mr. Hallmark was a genius
Much smarter than the Bard
'Cause Will just gave us poems and plays
Mr. H. – the greeting card!
It had to take a genius
To think it not absurd
That one would want to be expressed
In someone else's words.

Mr. Hallmark thought of everything
There's a card that you can get
For every occasion
Not a one did he forget
Yes, you can send a greeting
For every event
For Christmas, Easter, Chanukah
For Passover and Lent

For birthdays, showers, funerals
For weddings which display
Both straight and not straight couples
All unions are okay
'Cause matrimony's holy
And marriages are in
But just in case…there's something too
For those who live in sin

There are cards that say you hate him
There are cards that say you care
There are cards that say you're starting
Or ending an affair
There are cards that praise endowments
From toes up to the head
And cards where everyone shows off
How good they are in bed

There are cards that state you're moving
Or that you're staying put
And some that say your bird just died
That your marriage is kaput
There are even cards that tell you
What wines you should imbibe
But not a one have I yet found
Says, "Welcome to the tribe!"

So should we send an Elmo
Or maybe a Dalmatian
Perhaps some dancing rabbis
To lead the celebration?
No guidelines from the Hallmarks
We don't know what to do
So maybe we'll just tell you
We're glad that you're…well, you!

The Optimist

To see the glass half full all of the time
Is something only he can see and I'm
In awe of that which only he can do,
For by his optimism I've been touched too.

We know hope springs eternal in some breasts,
In him it doesn't spring, it rather nests,
The sun is always shining on his set,
There are no grays or blacks on his palette.

He won't let petty things get in his way,
He'll rise above it all, the noise, the fray,
The sky's the limit? He wants to know why.
If optimists live longer, then he'll never die.

The Poet

Yes, poets walk among us
And have since time began
Their works serve to inspire
Enrich the lives of men
Some sing of fields of daffodils
The mysteries of birds
And they can touch us with their gifts
The beauty of their words
They make us feel the turmoil
Of ships on oceans tossed
They make us know the anguish of
The damaged and the lost
We listen, for they see beyond
Above what others see
And they express the truths they glean
With grace and artistry
And you, you are a poet too
A different kind, it's true
But that so many stand and walk
Is often thanks to you
Your knowledge and your genius
Perfected a technique
That offers hope, an end to pain
For those with prospects bleak

Some poets they write villanelles
Some odes to lovers' lips
While you write with a different pen
You're a poet of the hips!

The Other Side
(A MELodrama)

We know Mel is brilliant, no doubt about that
Creator and planner, wears more than one hat
He started a School which was solely his vision
And then he went on to create a Division
He's principled, decent, outspoken, heroic
He's humble and fearless, persuasive and stoic
There's no one who's better as colleague or friend
And by now you can't wait for this bullshit to end!
Well, no, it's not bullshit, that he's all that is true
But that doesn't mean he's not other things too
And though there are many, in the interest of haste
We'll just pick a couple to give you a taste.

There's Mel the mechanic, alas, no technique
He can't hang a picture, he can't fix a leak
And often we wonder how such a big star
Can be felled in one swoop by a wee VCR
But we do have the proof, there are tapes, quite a horde
Filled with nothing but static, where Mel tried to record
There are other things too that pale his complexion
And that's anything that comes with directions
Assemblage he hates but still he will try
And it never works but he always knows why
And then he'll explain until we're all weary
Why it doesn't work, 'cause he's got the theory.

Then there's Mel, the talker, this is serious stuff
Too bad he can't tell when we've had enough
Oft' when Mel starts talking just watch our eyes glaze
This is what is known as suffering from MELaise
Yes, when Mel starts talking, our eyes will soon close
And before he's through, we'll be comatose
And even our grandson who naptime detests
When Mel's on the scene, gets plenty of rest

But that doesn't stop him in his dissertation
There's no need for Valium, he is our sedation
And there is no topic of which he can't sing
It seems he knows ALL about EVERYTHING!
And no use to argue 'cause try as you might
You never can win, Mel is ALWAYS right
And sooner or later he will wear you down
So when Mel starts talking, better just leave town.

Now that Mel's retiring, he needs more to do
So he started writing and he loves that too
And for us, his audience, this is pure delight
'Cause now he keeps talking about what he'll write
The topics of interest have changed o'er the years
Philosophy's big now, comes out of our ears
The richness of language, its color, its tone
He's smitten with words, they're mostly his own.

But now it is over and it's closing time
The end is the hardest, espeshly in rhyme
For tributes are due here, some words from the heart
But for that we will point you to the poem's start
Since, really, this night honors Mel's career life
He already knows the thoughts of his wife.
But, Mel, just a footnote, though sadness it bring
That perhaps, just perhaps, you don't know everything
Because, I believe, you hadn't a clue
That I was writing this poem for you.

To Seek or not to Seek?

So what conclusion should a reader reach
From reading ISABELLE wherein you teach
That every single great man of renown
Eventually is toppled and brought down
That every dreamer reaching for that star
Will fail and fall? – That's just the way things are.

Well, if that's true, as you more than imply
I'm only glad my sights aren't set that high.

Weep For Me
(To the tune of *I Get A Kick Out Of You*)

My story is much too sad to be told
'Cause practically everything leaves him totally cold
The only exception I know, though, is this,
When ensconced in his favorite nook,
With his pads and his pens and the Book,
On his face there's that ISABELLE look,
A look of pure bliss.

He gets no kick from champagne
Mere alcohol doesn't thrill him at all
There's only one thing that thrills Mel –
And that is his book, ISABELLE

He gets no kick from a play
Watching TV is a no-no for he
Has to be done by three or there's hell
And I'd like to kill ISABELLE

He gets a kick only when he sees those words accumulating
Six hundred pages long – if you please – while murder I'm
contemplating

What's worse, gets no kick from *moi*
And if I even stood nude, likely would
Still stay glued to that Brookhaven belle
So I plan to burn ISABELLE.

The Perfect Parent

The kind of parent I was going to be
Is the kind that's perfect with a capital P.
I would be warm, I would be gentle
I'd care for his needs both social and mental
We would communicate and not just talk
'Cause I'd have read both Freud and Spock
I'd give him love, I'd give him time
Oh, our relationship would be sublime
I'd be understanding, allow him to grow
And when he was ready, I'd let him go.
And I was that parent right up to the day
My child was born and got in the way.

A Labor Of Love
(To the tune of *The Battle Hymn of the Republic*)

The month was April and the year was 1959
And I went into labor for that happening divine
For on that day you were supposed to come, sweet son of mine
But you would not come out

Everybody watched and waited
Mel was getting aggravated
You were being complicated
You just would not come out

Three days of labor was no fun and caused Mel such distress
'Twould take you hours to appear, like seventy, more or less
So even in the womb you showed those signs of stubbornness
You just would not come out

You weren't going to be rushed, you made that very clear
And we'd just have to wait around, perhaps another year
Till you were good and ready, that's the time you would appear
You just would not come out

Already it was obvious that you'd be one of a kind
And we all wondered whether maybe you had changed your mind
But what was sure was that you were a pain in my behind
'Cause you would not come out

Things were getting pretty serious
Your delay was most mysterious
Mel was getting quite delirious
But you would not come out

A surgeon was consulted and he said he'd operate
There was no time to lose, he said, or it might be too late
And so they took you out or else it seemed you'd not vacate
You finally came out

Yes, finally you did come out and we all knocked on wood
And what a boy and what a man you grew into, so good
The envy of all others and of every neighborhood
You were worth waiting for

So this song is just for you-ou
'Cause today you're forty-two-oo
Where you are, we wish we knew-ew
But you don't tell us squat
And you never keep in tou-ouch
Things have not changed all that mu-uch
You don't visit us and su-uch
So when will you come out?

A Dreamer at Fifteen

My son wants to know the meaning of life
He's fifteen and longs to be cool
He searches his soul from morning till night
While I go to work to teach school

He's riddled with questions, "Is that all there is?"
Will life ever grant him his wishes?
He does this while casually watching TV
While I clean the house and wash dishes

He needs to experience, he needs to try out
He talks and he talks on and on
He wonders and ponders and makes such grand plans
While I do the garbage and lawn

The weight of the world on his shoulders it rests
He says so again and again
Yet the real heavy loads, he leaves them for me
While he sleeps each morning till ten

But I have stopped worrying, my son is okay
I know that his thinking's not hazy
'Cause whenever I opt to change places with him
He always says, "Are you crazy?"

Growing Up
(To the tune of *The Battle Hymn of the Republic*)

Well, Hal, since I have written 'bout your brother and your Dad
I think I owe the same to you or else you might be sad
So let me reminisce about the good times that we had
While you were growing up

That you were going to be tough was obvious, I suppose
You nixed the playpen, car seat, carriage – all things you'd oppose
And so I couldn't go and do my best thing – try on clothes
While you were growing up

But today you are a sta-ar
You have come from very fa-ar
Rare and well done's what you a-are
It wasn't always so

One day when I was bugging you, you put me in my place
We were out dining and you threw that burger in my face
We thought that you'd end up in jail 'cause crime you would embrace
And you were only four

Your teenage years, I wish I could forget how they were spent
Your fav'rite word was my least favorite – EXPERIMENT!
You tried it all, my patience too, for that was your intent
When you were growing up

But today you are a sta-ar
You have come from very fa-ar
Rare and well done's what you a-are
It wasn't always so

And then in 1982 for college you would leave
By then you were more liberal than Mel or I or Steve
And so when Reagan got elected, you could only grieve
There went your college years

And when I asked about your grades, you asked how I expected
That you could concentrate on school when Reagan got elected
How could I be so inhumane when you were so dejected
And feeling such great pain?

And pain was something that you felt for all humanity
You thought that we should help mankind – I don't think you meant me
I'd say, "Take out the garbage," and you'd say, "Three cans? All three?"
When you were growing up

But today you are a sta-ar
You have come from very fa-ar
Rare and well done's what you a-are
It wasn't always so

A nature lover from the start, the things you liked to do
Like hiking, climbing, camping were all things that we'd eschew
And you'd come back with poison oak and poison ivy too
When you were growing up

Then Israel and the kibbutz, you had to go and see
Your job o'er there was tending ducks and oft you'd say to me
"Mom, when they come to kill these birds, I'm gonna set them free"
I worried that you might

But today you are a sta-ar
You have come from very fa-ar
Rare and well done's what you a-are
It wasn't always so

Your int'rest in religion took us by surprise, 'twas news
'Cause that was something Mel and Steve and I would never choose
Of course, it centered more on Hindus, Buddhists than on Jews
When you were growing up

The best way to describe you then, anti-establishment
And we had trouble, often, understanding what you meant
E.g., you said, you'd wear no watch 'cause time's irrelevant
So you were always late

But today you are a sta-ar
You have come from very fa-ar
Rare and well done's what you a-are
It wasn't always so

Yes, that was then and this is now, today you're thirty-eight
That you are happy, there's no doubt, and no need for debate
You're not that diff'rent than you were but now we think that's great
I guess that we've grown up!

My Sons, Then and Now

My sons, when they were little long ago
Would not always behave, behave just so
Not everything was always so sublime
I did a lot of screaming in my time

Some of the things they did, I must confess
Got on my nerves, e.g. their rooms a mess
The unmade beds, the dishes in the sink
Their wounded pride, their sulks drove me to drink
And I was often nasty, in a snit
And let them know they were the cause of it

But now that they are grown, they're really great
I love their calls, our talks, how we relate
Yes, now that they are grown, they have no flaws
And I am wondering if that's because
They are much nicer for they've changed somehow
Or if it's *I* who am much nicer now

To a Father from his Mother

What your first words would be, we oft' debated
"Vector Analysis," a friend speculated
It seems that your daughter is not like her Dada
The first word *she* uttered – quite clearly – was Prada

Ode to a Grad

Well, dear Jo Ann, you've got it all
Great looks and brains to boot
An MBA, a Wall Street job
You'll soon be making loot
Yes, you worked hard to have it all
You organized and planned
And while I'm thrilled with your success
Pray tell, where is my Grand?

You care for Steve, you buy his clothes
Cholesterol you ban
You make appointments, cook and bake –
One hundred ways with bran
You call, you write, you exercise
I can't keep up with you
But didn't you forget one thing?
Pray tell, where's you know who?

Don't tell me that the answer is
You're really not that wild
About the thought of giving up
Your freedom for a child
To pick up after, feed and change
Lose sleep, be filled with doubt
And always, always worry 'bout
Just how *it* will turn out
I can't believe you just want fun
To fly so fancy free
And that you're not at all thrilled by
Being taught humility!

We're Very Good Friends, My Grandson and I

We're very good friends, my grandson and I
I can't wait for the weekend, to his house I will fly
In the gray BMW that he likes so well
We'll get there in no time, we're driven by Mel

So when we arrive, he jumps on my back
He can't wait to play but we have to unpack
How long will it take? We can't really tell
But probably long, we're unpacked by Mel

Then he wants to play, so we play, of course
Sometimes I'm a dog, sometimes I'm a horse
Sometimes we play cards, he knows no defeats
And he always wins but he *never* cheats!

We have lots of talks, my grandson and I
Of just how it was in years now gone by
We'd go to the park and feed ducks and birds
And I'd make up songs and change all the words
And I'd push him high, high up in the swing
And we'd sing those songs and boy, could he sing!

And so the day goes, soon it's time for bed
Now comes the best part, stories to be read
And he always says, "Please, read just one more,"
So I end up reading one, two, three and four

And he asks me questions, says he wants to know
What a word I read him means, the word is *beau*
And when I am finished saying what it is
He gives me that look and says that I am his

And I call him *darlin'* and he calls me Chris
And there's nothing quite like his goodnight kiss
And when we awake, downstairs we will go
And we'll look for *Skittles* but Mom mustn't know

And then comes that time I must say goodbye
He gets kind of sad, sometimes he will cry
And though he can't see what I try to hide
I am crying too but I cry inside

Because love can hurt, he'll find out one day
When you love so much, that's the price you pay
But I'll soon be back, so our tears we'll dry
And wait for that moment, my grandson and I!

Until Soon

We hung out all weekend, we had so much fun
'Cause I love Zack more than I love anyone
But then came the time that I had to go back
I always get sad when I have to leave Zack

We went to his game and he was, oh, so good
He put on my coat but said *No* to the hood
He's such fun to be with, he just has the knack
I always get sad when I have to leave Zack

We did some Vocab and real good was his mood
Translucent and *various, abundant* and *brood*
I'm sorry but I don't remember the rest
I sure hope that Zack gets an A on his test

We watched some TV and we learned a new word
Shepoopie, the funniest that we ever heard
But I wasn't laughing when I had to pack
I always get sad when I have to leave Zack

He played us the piano and boy, can he play
De Bussy and Liszt, I could listen all day
But I had to go then, alas and alack
I always get sad when I have to leave Zack

And Mom had bronchitis and Dad wasn't there
He was locked in his room on the speaker somewhere
And Ellie, the actress, would cut us no slack
Of course I got sad 'cause I had to leave Zack

So now I'm back home in my very own place
But all I can see is his cute little face
And the sun doesn't shine, there's no happy refrain
And I will be sad till I see Zack again

The Eliza Special

At 4:00 A.M the nightly drama
Eliza is crying, "I want my Mama!"
The darkness is pierced by horrible screams
Shattering sleep and everyone's dreams

Grandma Chris to the rescue but she won't be consoled
"I don't like your nightgown!" she'll holler and scold
"That kind's for the summer!" she'll scream and berate
My luck, my granddaughter is a fashion plate

And what better time her talents to show
Than at 4:00 in the morning but she won't let go
So I change my nightgown as per her request
But I'm still not Mama and so she can't rest

And at 4:00 A.M. something else becomes clear
Everyone around me must have a tin ear
For no matter how loud that toddler will yell
She won't get a rise out of Steve, Zack or Mel

So it's all up to me, there's no end in sight
Will I get her to sleep or will she win the fight?
"I want my Mama!" she continues her taunt
And the word that she stresses the loudest is WANT!

She maintains her stance, this nightmare in pink
And it's obvious to me that she will not blink
That I am no match for this ball of defiance
And Mel's fast asleep so there's no help from Science

I wish I could say it was something I said
Or did that finally gets her to bed
She decides to lie down and with trembling chin
Says, "Chris, sleep with me," and invites me in

And she drinks her milk while curling my hair
And tells me exactly how to lie and where
And though I don't do it just like Mama *dooz*
She is calming down and beginning to snooze

When she wakes the next morning, she's no longer mad
And I'm the best Grandma that she's ever had
Everything's forgotten from the night before
Once more her angelic status is restored

As for me, I'll remember and look back on this
As another "wild night" for her Grandma Chris!

Thoroughly Modern Eliza

In a house like no other in Scarsdale N...Y...
Where beautiful flowers abound and birds fly
Not far from the duck pond, the park and the track
Lives lovely Eliza and her big brother Zack.

And Ellie is special, a rare little girl
You'll find no eyes bluer and no blonder curl
A smile that will melt you and win you, no doubt,
And then hold you captive, so better watch out!

And don't think that beauty is all that she's got.
That's one modern woman that three-year-old tot
And though she likes Barbies and everything pink
She has lots of gray cells, Eliza can think.

She's just the right mixture of solid and fluff
She loves dressing up but she sure knows her stuff
She counts and she spells and she sings and plays games
She knows all the dinosaurs, all of their names

And knows which is which, oh, much better than you
So you better learn them 'cause she'll quiz you too
And if there should be one whose name you don't know
She'll get quite indignant and she'll tell you so.

She loves all her books and will ask you to read
But don't try to fool her 'cause you won't succeed
She knows every word there and boy she keeps track
If you try to skip one, she'll make you go back.

But don't you go thinking all work and no play
'Cause she and her brother can run wild all day
The energy level's sky-high, that's the truth
She once fell so hard, she lost part of her tooth.

And when not in motion but firm on the ground
In front of a mirror our girl can be found
Where make up and *li-stick* and creams she'll apply
And you won't know whether to laugh or to cry.

Then come the long dresses, the hats, the high heels
And her deepest secrets to you she reveals
As well as her wishes, here's what she'll confide –
That what she'd like most to be is a bride.

And if the occasion should ever arise
When you're asked to guess how she is disguised
And you say, a princess, the fairest you've seen
She'll quickly correct you and say she's a queen.

So that is Eliza, the crème de la crème
A beauty, a brain, a beguiler, a gem
And this story's over, it's all that I've got
But I'd like to end it with this final thought:

If ever you had to decide which is best
The one thing you cherish above all the rest
It would be quite easy to pick, the best part
Is hearing, "I love you with all of my heart."
But though very tempting, alas, truth it lacks
You know she can't mean it. Her heart's clearly Zack's.

We Think That Zack and Ellie Should Be Friends

(To the tune of *The Farmer and the Cowman Should Be Friends*)

We think that Zack and Ellie should be friends
Oh, we think that Zack and Ellie should be friends
Zackie likes his cars to race, El likes makeup on her face
But that's no reason why they can't be friends

Brothers and sisters should stick together
To get along should always try
They shouldn't tease or hurt each other
And never make each other cry

I'd like to say a word for our Zackie
Behind those gorgeous eyes there's something cooking
No matter what his toy, Ellie's brings him much more joy
And so he helps himself when no one's looking

We think that Zack and Ellie should be friends
We think that Zack and Ellie should be friends
Ellie likes her princess clothes, Zack likes anything that goes
But that's no reason why they can't be friends

Brothers and sisters should stick together
To get along should always try
They shouldn't tease or hurt each other
And never make each other cry

I'd like to say a word for Eliza
The angel that she is and like no other
She's just one perfect kid, does no wrong, but if she did
You may be sure she'd blame it on her brother

Brothers and sisters should stick together
To get along should always try
They shouldn't tease or hurt each other
And never make each other cry

For there will come a day in the future
When they will leave their mother and their father
They'll go out on their own but they'll never be alone
'Cause if they get along, they'll have each other

Brothers and sisters should stick together
To get along should always try
They shouldn't tease or hurt each other
And never make each other cry

If Ever We Should See You

(To the tune of *If Ever I Would Leave You*)

If ever we should see you
It wouldn't be in Summer
'Cause Summer is a bummer
And you have no time
You're flying, you're running
New York to L.A.
You're busy us shunning
But what can we say?

If ever we should see you
It wouldn't be in Fall
'Cause Fall is not at all
A time to see us
You're running, you're flying
You make our heads spin
Sometimes you will call us
Never when we're in.

Alas there is no morning, there is no noon, no night
No day, no week, no month, not ever when the time is right

If ever we should see you
It wouldn't be in Spring
In Spring you're in Bejing
Or Paris or Seoul
Or London or Rome
Your trail's sometimes cold
You're never at home
And we're getting old.

If ever we should see you
It wouldn't be in Winter
Because we know in Winter
You're never around
You're running, you're flying
Who knows what you do?
But we're not implying
That we wish we knew.

Alas there is no morning, there is no noon, no night
No day, no week, no month, not ever when the time is right

If ever we should see you
It wouldn't be this Season
A season's not a reason
To see Mom and Dad
Those folks, you remember
The ones gave you birth
Your family members
Have they lost their worth?

If ever we should see you
I don't think we would know you
"When did you get your nose fixed?"
Is what we would ask
And what would we tell you?
Just what would we say?
We'd probably ask why
You're not in L.A.

Other Cities, Other Rooms

When did you get to be a man, my son?
It must have happened when I wasn't looking
You slipped out of your Doctor Denton's, your school books under
your arm
Into a man in a business suit
The weight of New York City on your frail, over-exercised shoulders
Talking of leaving it, moving on

I sleep in your and your wife's bed in a lovely room overlooking that city
And I remember all the rooms where you slept in mine
On Plamondon, on Blydenburgh, on Orbit Drive
And I marvel at the transition
At the man you have become
At my love for you
Here in New York City, or in rooms elsewhere
For that cord of long ago is forever intact

The Visit

We come to visit you, our darling Zack
We've made the trip to your Camp Mah-Kee-Nac
We watch you and your Iroquois play ball
And see that you have slimmed down and grown tall

As ever gorgeous with that skin, those eyes
That soon those squealing girls will idolize
I know you don't believe when this I say
But mark my words, soon they won't run away

You take us by the hand, you are our guide
You show us what your bunk looks like inside
And then you lead us to your favorite spot
The lakefront in the breeze where it's less hot

"It's peaceful here," you say and it's so right
How can a nine year old's words be so bright?
You look out at the water's silvery hue
And I glimpse that poetic side of you

And when we talk, it's absolutely clear
That you have become wise beyond your years
Trying to solve your problems on your own
Which can be hard even for one who's grown

And then it's lunch, a rest, a perfect day
But soon we'll have to leave, to go away
For visiting is over, we must part
But visiting is never over in my heart

Advice

The passing on to future generations
Of what through our experience we have learned
Is simply futile. Our recommendations
And all our help and wisdom will be spurned.

Our children say they know what they are doing
That we should let them make their own mistakes
And oh, they will, they will, that's what we're ruing
Because we know they have just what it takes.

So if your daughter dates below her station
And brings home Juan, a gardener, for romance
Do not bring up her Harvard education
Or that she is allergic to most plants.

And if your son is into transcendental
And so must heed the Maharishi's call
Do not remind him that he's Occidental
That he descends from Abraham and Saul.

You do not want to see your children suffer
And so you often run off at the mouth
Your daughter wants no part of what you offer
And just might take her Juan and move down South.

And when your son brings home his latest cutie
And you are sure that he has lost his mind
Don't ask, "Why's her hair pink?" It's not your duty
And keep remembering that love is blind.

So don't expect that your children will hear you
The chance of that is really very small
The more you talk, the less it will endear you
The only thing's to catch them when they fall.

Death on the Tracks

I didn't know you
Though once, I too had children
And with all mothers I grieve your deaths
But wait, there are questions
So many questions that we need answered
What was it that drove you to those tracks
On that chill December afternoon –
When you should have been dancing
Or talking on the phone
Or fixing your hair –
To lay down your young lives
Your dreams, your future?
What kind of pain was it that could not be endured
That made you want to end it all
And to do it so finally and so well?

You are gone
But the questions remain
Unanswered
And we will never know
Because, even if you could
You could not tell us.

A Cut Above

Oh, how the years have hastened
Since first you cut my hair
So many Saturdays have gone
And you were always there.

I'd travel many miles for
That haircut so sublime
Your scissors have been silenced.
There will be no next time.

The ones who now will cut me
The Juans and the Miguels
Will charge me twice as much but
Will not do half as well.

And I will always miss you
There's no one will compare
From now on it's the angels
Who'll have the finest hair.

He Cried Alone

He was a brother, one of three
And fate had dealt him a sad hand
His life was cloaked in mystery
One that we could not understand

And yet he lived, did not complain
And did not ask too much of those
Who wished to help him in his pain,
Did not demand, did not impose

And did not, in this day and age
Of mine, mine, mine, and me, me, me
Ever desire center stage
He lived his life more quietly

Compared to others, this may not
Be very much, yet it should be
For it can mean an awful lot
To all those who are left guilt-free

What then should his epitaph be?
What should be written on his stone?
He never burdened anyone –
And if he cried, he cried alone.

Blue in the Night

Mamma,
You went so gentle into that good night
You never fought the dimming of the light
And I who watched you, helpless, slip away
Could offer nothing that would make you stay.

Regret

A hamburger at McRory's
With onions, you liked it so much
And wanted me so to come with you
But I was too busy for such

And bridge at the clubs, how it beckoned
You'd gotten to be quite a pro
You'd ask me if I'd be your partner
But I was too busy to go

If only, if only, if only
If I could correct each mistake
But death won't allow for do-overs
'Cause life gives us only one take

How well I remember those moments
But now they bring only distress
You asked me for so very little
I managed to give even less

Regret and deep sorrow I feel now
In dreams oft I turn and I toss
I never sang for you, Mother
Years later I'm feeling the loss

My Mother, Myself
a dream

You were old and frail and somewhat confused
It was winter in Montreal
And I wanted to buy you a warm coat and shoes

In the clothing store, you walked over to a rack
And smiling at me playfully picked out
A swanky sweater and sandals
Open in front and back
And like a child, sat down in an overstuffed chair
And happily started rocking back and forth

I looked at what you had chosen
Impractical reminders of a different past
And without uttering a word
Readily bought them for you
Remembering all the times we'd be shopping for me
And you'd do the same

The Return

There was a time when you, my son, my son
Were deeply troubled, self-destructive too,
You found no solace, not in anyone,
And in the end, what could I do for you?
The reasons why, they do not matter now,
Nor did they then, as I very well knew,
I could do nothing, I did not know how,
The fault lay in the stars and not in you.
And so I watched your sad decline and fall –
It broke my heart, as it will those who care –
And I grew sick as darkness covered all,
I could not lift you out of your despair.
That you wanted to die, of that I'm sure,
That you no longer do has proved my cure.

Sister

Conceived in hope but born into a hell,
You'd not open your eyes or take a breath.
It was as if you sensed it, you could tell
That if you lived, 'twould mean our certain death.
And so you gave your life for ours that day –
What day? What place? Nobody ever said –
You just removed yourself and went your way
And freed us for the road that lay ahead.
If you had lived, if there had been no war,
We would have loved each other through and through,
Told stories, laughed and danced and so much more –
Instead, this constant ache of missing you.
Today I cry for all that could have been,
For you, our stillborn little heroine.

The First Night

Monday 1:30 AM
You are gone less than twenty-four hours
And here in your bed which I have chosen
I cannot, I will not sleep
Oh, dearest father
What is it that hurts so much
What is it that will not let me rest
Will I ever be myself again

You lived inside me
Around me
In my heart
In my mind
For fifty-nine years
How can a single rip in the fabric
Your breathing stopped
Your eyes closed after death
Rob me of you
Leave me so incomplete
So wanting
And yet how can it not

The connections are deep
The threads intertwined
Intricately
Irrevocably
Undeniably
You were here and now you're not
I will never be whole again

A Winter Memory

(Montreal, 1949)

Maybe it's just the way I remember it
Maybe it's only nostalgia and nothing more
But I wish you could know
That I always felt privileged
That I lacked for nothing
Even when we moved from room to rented room
And I helped you pull that sled
On which rested our entire fortune
The wicker trunk holding the sum total of our precious belongings
Here on Earth

Small Comfort

I think of you, dear mother, father
As this new war I'm going through
My thoughts return me to the other
The one that we three so well knew

Six million gone, so many ours
Your sisters, brothers, parents too
The victims of those other towers
Of other lunatics' world-view

So now again, in this great nation
Where things like this don't happen – war
And loss and grief and devastation
And fear of all that was before

The horror lingers, it keeps growing
It will not leave, it will not go
But I take comfort in the knowing
That you're no longer here to know

They Didn't Make a Lampshade out of Me

(To the tune of *Act Naturally*)

They were gonna put me in the ovens
They were gonna hang me from a tree
They were gonna gas me in their chambers
They were gonna make a lampshade out of me

They were gonna put me in their boxcars
They were gonna murder me with glee
They were gonna bury me still breathing
They were gonna make a lampshade out of me

Oh yes, they wanted to destroy me
Annihilate, expunge my progeny
But I outlasted every bastard
And while they're pushing daisies, I walk free

Oh no, they didn't kill my spirit
They left me ears to hear and eyes to see
They left my voice intact so I can tell you
They didn't make a lampshade out of me

PART III The Tackan Years

A Model School

Each year I resolve myself to improve
Which really isn't such a bad move
We all know it's good to try to aspire
To set our goals a little bit higher
But where I believe I make a mistake
Is in those that for my models I take.
Why does a role model have to be a star
Someone who's admired only from afar?
Is the Broadway stage the best that there is?
Are the finest clothes only worn by Liz?
Do the folks at Harvard have the finest minds?
Do the Playboy bunnies have the best behinds?
Or are there perhaps – if I look around –
Many fine examples right here to be found?
Well, there's Mery F with her fashion sense
And there's Lois L with her confidence
And there's Judy C who knows all the facts
Bonnie Smiles can teach us all how to relax
Karen Veit can tell us what to do with fleas
Ursula can pick out all our Christmas trees –
She can't bring them here, of that there's no doubt
Because if she does, Lex will throw them out –
Then there's Winie Ching, expert on all books
And Grace has no peers among turkey cooks
Rose is the best shopper, gets gifts by the barrel
And who can do coffee better than our Carol?
Elaine's a prop maker, she can build the ark
So what if her whale looked more like a shark?
Carol B's a ham, she can teach us how

Pat's a decorator – order your wreaths now –
Diane's still our mentor, our right brains she guards
And at each dismissal holds up idiot cards
Nancy wants to learn and she does with ease
Yes, she quests for knowledge, as well as her keys
To keep us in shape we have Ron and June
And we have John Brocco to keep us in tune
Terry and Eileen, always of good cheer
Karen Piersanti… does she still teach here?
Then we have Joyce Miller who knows how to sing
And, of course, there's Bill who knows EVERYTHING!
And from Pat, our boss, we learn things each day –
Bulletin boards change but who'll do a play?
Actually Pat is cool, takes things on the chin
But those *suspicious incidents* they just might do her in.
So I think that it's obvious, with talent we abound
Yes, there are many qualities in the people we're around
And as for me, I'm tricky, I think that's plain to see
Because I wrote four hundred words and not one about me!

Who's In First?

At Tackan these days there is only one fear
Who will be teaching what grade next year?
The grapevine is heavy with gossip so rare
That you won't need a perm, it'll curl your hair
Everyone has versions of how we'll be shifted
But no one knows reasons, not even the gifted
The place to avoid, the place that's the pits
Is the dear old mailbox 'cause that's where it sits
The little note that says, "Teacher Dear,
Please see me re placement for the coming year."
We circle that mailbox aquiver and pale
And some of us even have sent back our mail
But if the mailbox is cause for panic
The inner office is like the Titanic
One teacher fainted, three others prayed
"Oh Lord, please keep me in the same grade."
Some developed hives and have quite an itch
Others said that they'd rather fight than switch
Some were very cool and maintained their stance
They offered their bodies, they still have a chance.
But I know for sure, no one need be torn
Because guess who else got a note this morn
Yes, the boss himself! It said, "Barry Dear,
Please see me about placement for next year
Here at Central Office, new research has found
That it's best to move principals around
So we threw the dice and you lost the toss
My condolences. Signed, Pete A, your boss."

Five Santas, Three Wreaths, Two Dreidels, One Menorah and Still Counting

'Twas a week before Christmas and what do we see
In the Teachers' Room? A Christmas tree!
No one would admit to bringing it in
But we have our spies, so watch out, Eileen!
It looked kind of puny and quite underfed
But it was enough to make some see red
And so the next day, upon all the tables
There was Hanukah candy and a lot of dreidels
(There would have been more, I heard Cheryl say
But lucky for us, hers had lost their way)
Still and all, it seemed like an even score
Till the decorations hit the walls and door
There were seven Santas, there were reindeer three
But just one menorah was all I could see
And as if that wasn't enough cruelty
The menorah was blocked by the Christmas tree!
So I knew the next day, Lex would bring more candy
But no, I was wrong, latkes brought in Sandy
Well, I guess Pat Mulhall couldn't let that go
Next day 'neath the tree, she was adding snow
And I guess deciding that it looked so fine
She added two Santas, so now we have nine
At that point I thought there is nothing else
That's when Urs and Carol came in wearing bells!
So what else is out there that we need to fear?
A ten-foot menorah? Just wait till next year!
But for now there's peace, let us all be jolly
Still, to deck the halls, make sure you use... cholly!

Fourteen Carrot Snack

The other day at snack time
We witnessed something weird
For there before our very eyes
Our teacher disappeared
She wasn't drinking water
Or any purple stuff
She was just eating carrots
She'd had more than enough.

"The teacher's gone!" said Lisa
"No kidding, duh!" said Scott
And Heather said, "Let's find her!"
And Ben said, "Maybe not."
Danielle said, "Get the doctor!"
"No, get the nurse!" yelled Sue
And Paul said, "Get the blowpops!
I think she's coming to!"

And Justin said, "Let's party!"
And Chris said, "No! Let's blast!"
And then a voice familiar
Said, "Children, not so fast"
And James said, "Gee, where are you?
Why did you go away?
But since it seems you've vanished
Will we have Math today?"

We walked toward her voice to
The corner by the wall
And there we saw those lashes
On a carrot five feet tall!
So now we tell the story
Of Mrs. Month's demise
She turned into a carrot
Right there before our eyes!

Dear Little Children
(To the tune of *Little Buttercup*)

You sweet little children, you dear little children
You're leaving us now, it's good-bye
You dear little children, you sweet little children
We'll miss you and that is no lie.

We tried hard to teach you, we hope that we reached you
We always, yes always, were nice
There's no one as clever. Did we holler? Never!
Well, maybe just once or twice.

So come back and face us but please don't disgrace us
We really don't ask for that much
Just excellent scholars with plenty of dollars
And doctors and lawyers and such.

So bye, all you children, you dear little children
Remember the things that we taught
And also remember that here in September
We'll miss you, we liked you – a lot.

Rachel, Dear

I read your poem three times, Rachel, dear
And even after all those times, a little tear
And not just 'cause you write so beautifully
But that you chose to write so, about me
Because, if what you say is really true
It's just the thing I tried so hard to do
To give with the 3R's a little heart
The blowpops and the games were just a part.

And I remember also, oh I do
The one who made it tough to make it through
But we survived and in a decent way
Amazing, though, I didn't run away
'Cause I had lots of help, including you
That lovely, longhaired redhead in Row Two.

And so in closing, I just want to say
You really, really, really made my day
And I would like to tell you, as gifts go
Yours meant much more to me than you can know.

Language, Whole Language and Nothing but Whole Language

The year was 1992
And many things transpired
Bill Clinton won – he's President
And old George Bush got fired
The Russians are no longer foes
The Berlin Wall is down
But nothing topped *this* great event –
Whole Language came to town.

And many things are on the outs –
Dan Quayle and all his kin
Buchanan, Duke and Robertson –
But Houghton Mifflin's in
Yes, Houghton Mifflin's here to stay
We're all quite sure of it
And so we all gave up Thoreau
We're reading Children's Lit.

Yes, we're all reading Children's Lit
We all gave up the bard
And all our books now come in threes
They're easy, medium, hard
And we each have a manual
That weighs at least a ton
In which we can't find anything
And which is just part one.

And we all read that manual
No time to do our chores
'Cause we're collecting similes
And even metaphors
And when we go to sleep at night
We're so well trained, it seems
That all our dreams and fantasies
Unfold themselves in themes.

We're building background, teaching words
Preparing what we'll say
The kids just want to know one thing
"D'you think we'll read today?"
"You want to read? But I'm not done,"
I'm being really strict
"Stop asking foolish questions, child
Just sit there and predict."

The foreplay's over, this is it
For reading they're all poised
With partners, shared, cooperative
My fav'rite kind of noise
And when they finish, I'll discuss
The questions in those squares
And then they'll write, respond, create
Of course, they'll be in pairs.

Those little squares of red and green
They're making my head spin
Is there a question in the world
That's not contained therein?
But I'm compelled to do them all
These squares obsess me so
I'm now on Green Square twenty-five
I still have ten to go.

As for my kids, they've tuned me out
For squares they've no respect
Whether they're green for *author's craft*
Or red – *cause and effect.*
I'm finished now, the theme is done
I followed every step
And in my mark book are their grades
They're IND, GS or DEP.

Well, here I am in deep manure
And I've been here before
A roast without a toast is bad
I'll even up the score
Now if I sound too critical
Deep down I'm really not
I like Whole Language, and some parts
I even like a lot.

The days of Dick and Jane are gone
And change can't be denied
Not in our homes or schools or world
We cannot stem the tide
So let us hope that '93
Will see us look ahead
To friendly staff development
And kids who are well read.

Standards Are A-Coming to Town

(To the tune of *Santa Claus Is Coming to Town*)

You better watch out
You might wanna cry
You might wanna shout
We're telling you why
Standards are a-coming to town.

The Commissioner *knows*
What young kids can do?
Well, we're here to say
He hasn't a clue
Standards are a-coming to town.

We now have trouble sleeping
At night we lie awake
Those rubrics make us crazy
Like the plans we have to make.

They'd have us believe
They've made us aware
That what we once taught
Was full of hot air
Standards are a-coming to town.

The pressure is high
We're all getting sick
The kids could care less
They're still just as thick
Standards are a-coming to town.

We're making those damn rubrics
We put them on a chart
But could someone please tell us
How will that make kids smart?

There are other things
That seem as absurd
How can kids debate?
They can't spell the word
Standards are a-coming to town.

But judging by past
Experience we know
Those standards will come
Those standards will go
Standards are a-coming to town.

Will we survive the pressure?
Will we escape our ruts?
Will we continue normal?
Or will we all go nuts?

So maybe the way
To go is to quit
Incentive looks good
Enough of this...stuff
Standards come, we're saying bye, bye,
Standards come, we're saying bye, bye.

The Observation Tango
(To the tune of *La Cumparsita*)

Observations
Oh, how we love those observations
After we make our reservations
We're in a state of palpitations
And when you show up at our stations
We hope we'll meet your expectations
But if we don't, who cares, dear Lou?
We've taught longer than you!

Thirty yea-ears
We've done this crap for thirty yea-ears
And you're still wet behind the ea-ears
So why are *we* the ones with fea-ears?
No more! We'll dry those silly tea-ears
And when at our door you appea-ears
We'll welcome you with these words, boss
"Lou, why don't you get lost?"

The Play's the Thing

The school year began all virtue, no vice
I thought there's no poem, everything is too nice –
The morning bus duty is going just fine
We're all in our rooms at twenty past nine
We all have our workbooks, the schedule is swell
And *grievance* is only a tough word to spell
We still all are married to our last year's spouse
And Barbara, thank God, has at last sold her house
Even Lois calmed down, you don't hear her scream
Except at dismissal where she still reigns supreme
And Joyce with her music has shown us anew
That at heart we're all hams, whether Gentile or Jew.

But since by the cover you can't judge the book
I decided to take a much closer look
And under the surface, I noticed things stirring
So here are a few to which I'm referring:
Poor Bill hates third grade, he does nothing but grieve
But Urs'la likes fifth and says she won't leave
Elaine says she's fine, that first grade was her choice
But no one can hear her, she keeps losing her voice
And Karen Piersanti is turning real mean
'Cause Barry has hidden our ditto machine
And he will not tell us just where it did go
It's over the rainbow for all that we know
Pat Mulhall is furious, the wreath on her door
Was religious, not secular so it hangs there no more
But Pat won't stay down, she was born to rebel
So she's wearing a wreath in every lapel
And where's Judy L? Is she out of town
Until things religious have here settled down?
Or is she at home cutting out just the kind

Of reading material that will sure snap Pat's mind?
And Grace is annoyed and to Jack she won't speak
'Cause there's been no vacation or fur coat this week
And even on Joyce we can see signs of strain
'Cause the Wizard has said *whipperthnapper* again
And roar is the one thing the lion can't do
And Joan Bruno's mother will probably sue
And how come the boss, who as we all heard
Thinks that *competition* is a dirty word
And who never fails this to let us know
Is trying from Bill to steal the whole show?
But look here, you two, you don't stand a chance
Lois took a sick day just to learn her dance.

So we have our mess, that we can't deny
But what does it mean and what truths apply?
Perhaps we should view the play as the thing
That to all this mess will some meaning bring
The Wizard of Oz is not just a play
It resembles life in many a way:
Some might need a brain, some might need a heart,
Where them do we get? Yes where do we start?
No need to look more, it's simple because
Barry is our Wiz, Tackan is our Oz
And every so oft', 'cause of what we do
Children here do learn and dreams do come true.

The Grab Bag Blues

They were out of purple ice cream
They were out of hot pink hose
They were out of little decals
That you glue upon your toes

They were out of feather jewelry
They were out of boa belts
They were out of ten-inch earrings
Made of tiny rabbit pelts

They had no fluorescent knickers
And as hard as I might try
I could find no short, short dresses
That came up above the thigh

So I rushed home to my kitchen
And I baked a chocolate mousse
And I hope that you'll forgive me
If it's brown and not chartreuse

Let There Be Heat

When God created Man
He tried to be humane
He gave each one the things he'd need
Including, yes, a brain
But when the brains were being passed out
One fellow left his seat
And that's the man who's now in charge
Of fixing Tackan's heat.

Since then these men have multiplied
And now there's quite a crew
They come to Tackan once a week
Don't ask me what they do
They mostly knock and bang and hiss
And sure make quite a din
But when they leave, it's just as cold
As when they first came in.

So if there's someone out there
With a Harvard PhD
Or some super brilliant genius
From Yale or MIT
Who really wants a challenge
Who's bored with Shaw and Keats
Let him come down to Tackan
And try to fix our heats.

'Cause it won't be the inflation
It won't be World War III
It won't be rising taxes
Or nuclear energy
No, these are not the problems
That someday won't be solved
They will, I'm sure, and long before
We here stop being cold!

The Early Bird Catches the Bulletin Board

While we're still in bed
Covered up to our necks
And no one's in school –
Except maybe Lex –
Sheila Brodsky *is* here
With tape, glue and cord
She's decorating
Her bulletin board

And it's pumpkins and turkeys
And holiday lights
And poems and pictures
And shamrocks and kites
They're always so timely
And always just so
And always so clever
And so a propos

So I just want to thank her
And hope she'll pursue it
Because if she doesn't
I might have to do it!

We Did It Your Way
(To the tune of *I Did It My Way*)

And now, the end is here
And so we face the final curtain
Dear Pat, we'll say it clear
We'll state our case of which we're certain
We had a year that's full
We traveled each and every highway
And more, much more than this
We did it your way.

Regrets, we've had a few
But then again too few to mention
We did what you had us do
And saw it through without exemption
We planned each PARP event
Red Ribbon week in such a sure way
Not once did we complain
We did it your way.

But there were times we're sure you knew
When you bit off more than we could chew
Yet through it all when there was doubt
We ate it up and spit it out
We faced it all and we stood tall
We did it your way.

We juggled all the balls
We had our fill, our share of extras
We tried to keep them up
But we are not ambidextrous
To think we did all that
And never in an immature way
Oh no, oh no, not us
We did it your way.

But now that we've complained
You've turned around and shown some pity
Though what you planned for us
Just seems to be death by committee
Who wants to wake at dawn
To come talk here in some obscure way
Oh, gee, is it too late
To do it your way?

Two Retirements, One Leave of Absence
(Where does that put us on the seniority list?)

All great men have something that makes them unique –
A skill, a talent or perhaps their physique
When we think of Newton, we think of the apple
For Michelangelo, it's the Sistine Chapel
If it's bifocals, we think of Ben
And if it's Bo Derek, we think of a ten
If it's Swan Lake, it's very tofsky
Because there's nothing that rhymes with Tchaikovsky.

Now here in school, it's the same old story
We all have something that brings us glory:
For Karen, it's mice and spiders and bees.
For Nancy, it's courses – she has ten degrees
She's still missing one, a degree in rowing
It's given in Lapland, Nancy is going.
For Barbara, it's cooking that makes her an ace
You're looking for sugar? You're in the wrong place
There's one other thing that here you won't find –
A Basal Reader of any kind.
For Bill, we all know it's his sense of humor
But he's even better at starting a rumor
And as for Grace, it's a long, long tale
Of charge cards and showers and I hope not jail.
Giving orders, demanding and just a bit loud
Could only describe one teach in this crowd
Well, up to this year, *one* might have been true
But since September, alas there are two
Who shares this honor? I'll never tell
But their first initials are B and L.
And who for her brains? Diane is the one
Because she can do what no one else can
She's the only one here who's never in doubt
That she knows what Barry is talking about.
And what's Barry doing behind that closed door?

He's writing Memo One-Hundred-Four
Or studying research with titles that muse
How is a hot dog like yesterday's news?
And I'd like to tell him but perhaps not now
That nobody really wants to know how
But I can't upset him because it's quite clear
That Barry is suffering from Pep Tests this year
And I hope by next year those test scores are met
Or a peptic ulcer Barry might get.

For Doris, it's gardens and plants and French bread
But not after seven 'cause then she's in bed
She does many things but the one she does best
Is getting nightly twelve hours of rest.
One day I noticed that Doris was rude
And I inquired about her mood
'Cause Doris is always so sweet and polite
She said, *I slept only ten hours last night.*
I once phoned Doris at six o'clock
And was told by her husband that she couldn't talk
I asked why and he said she was out for the night
I said, *Out on the town?* He said, *Out like a light!*

Gloria isn't here, she had to go home
She probably knew I was writing this poem
Or maybe she's doing what she does most right –
Videotaping every program in sight.
I once told Gloria a-way back when
That I was planning to study Zen
I needed a book called *The Mind and Its Shape*
She said, *Don't buy it, I've got it on tape!*
So Gloria is home taping something juicy
Let's see… Thursday night… must be reruns of *Lucy.*

Now it's your turn, Robin. Is she still here?
And you I've been studying for many a year
You don't like traffic, you can't stand a crowd
You don't like the city, you say it's too loud
If it's too dirty, you don't like the joke
And all of us know how you feel about smoke
Your energy level, you claim, is too low
But your taxes are high and so is the snow
The shopping is bad and so is the news
And the stores on Long Island don't have your size shoes
The clothes in the mall are too cheap or too old
You suffer from burnout or else you're too cold
Your kitchen is yellow and you want it bluish
You kvetch and you kvetch, are you sure you're not Jewish?

If the way I have painted my colleagues so far
Makes them look one-sided, that's not what they are.
So Bernie and Lois, please don't flip your lids
You know we admire what you do with the kids.
And if there are others who feel I abuse
Just think of yourselves as a poet's muse
And don't be angry 'cause according to rumor
Everything is fair in love, war and humor.
One does not agree and I doubt he will
Bernie is sending me looks that could kill
But such a good friend one never forsakes
As long as he gives those long music breaks.

So now, Robin, Doris and Gloria, adieu
It's been a real pleasure here working with you
We wish you the best, write a note, give a call –
Oh, and Glo, send a tape – you'll be missed by us all.

If We Only Had a Brain

(To the tune of *If I Only Had a Brain*)

Would we come here every day
Where kids just wanna play
Where all we do's in vain?
We'd go elsewhere and be lazy
Where the kids don't make us crazy
If we only had a brain.

Would we be in this position
This Spanish Inquisition
This daily dose of pain –
Where each John, Jane and Freddy
Makes us scream, "Enough already!" –
If we only had a brain?

Oh, we could be so free
At home or at the shore
We could do the things
We never could before
Like sleep and shop
And shop some more.

We could while away the hours
And plan more baby showers
Or take a trip to Maine
We would not be a jerk
We would not show up for work
If we only had a brain.

On a cruise to the Bahamas
On safaris to hunt llamas
We all would surely go
We'd have babies, we'd retire
And we'd just sit by the fire
If we only had the dough!

Our Favorite Things
(To the tune of same)

Red Ribbon Week, Multicultural too
Health Walk, Parade, PARP is all that we do
The circus strong man and monkeys on swings
These are a few of our favorite things.

Latkes and strudel and tacos and knishes
Jewish, Italian and Mexican dishes
Sushi and turkey and cranberry rings
These are a few of our favorite things.

When we're bored nights
When the dog bites
When we're feeling sad
We simply remember our favorite things
And then we don't feel so bad.

Everyone's happy and busily eating
Oh, oh, we didn't have time left for Reading
Maybe tomorrow, let's see what it brings
Probably more of our favorite things.

More celebrations, oh boy, are we lucky
No time for Math but who cares Math is yucky
Instead, assemblies where everyone sings
These are a few of our favorite things.

When we're bored nights
When the dog bites
When we're feeling sad
We simply remember our favorite things
And then we don't feel so bad.

Pull-outs and push-ins, computers, we're giddy
No time to get down to the nitty-gritty
Health and Enrichment and Trumpets and Strings
These are a few of our favorite things.

Workshops and concerts, our life is so full
Another night we'll be spending in school
Reading to grown-ups about frogs and kings
These are a few of our favorite things.

When we're bored nights
When the dog bites
When we're feeling sad
We simply remember our favorite things
And then we don't feel so bad.

Pressure is building and everything bothers
Everyone's kvetching but some more than others
"No Whining" signs decorating both wings
These are a few of our favorite things.

Another kickoff will soon be upon us
Into another deal someone will con us
The Science Expo! We're spreading our wings!
These are a few of our favorite things.

When we're bored nights
When the dog bites
When we're feeling sad
We simply remember our favorite things
And then we don't feel so bad.

What's this we hear? No, it cannot be so
Full is the calendar, D-Day must go
Oh, how depressing and oh, how it stings
Losing the best of our favorite things.

When we're bored nights
When the dog bites
When we're feeling sad
We simply remember our favorite things
And then we don't feel so bad.

Barry's Way

You told me to be a risk-taker
To vary my style and my pace
So I did as you suggested
And I fell flat on my face.

You told me not to use dittoes
It's activities that make the kids think
So I did as you suggested
And the noise nearly drove me to drink.

You told me to use different methods
Even old dogs can learn a new trick
So I did as you suggested
But I also developed a tic.

You told me to try biofeedback
To learn what I'm all about
So I did as you suggested
But I hate what I found out.

You told me to do problem solving
It helps to make the mind strong
Now everyone's solving problems
But all the answers are wrong.

You said, "It's the process, not product"
Or is it the other way round?
I never remember the difference
For there is no difference, I found.

You said, "Individualization"
I'm never to teach the whole class
So I split myself right down the middle
It's really a pain in the... neck.

You said SOI was the latest
And you should know, you're the boss
But whenever I bring up the subject
People always ask if it's sauce.

I really respect your opinion
I think I could learn lots from you
But do you mind just one question?
Is *anything* right that I do?

Well really, you don't have to answer
So just put that question on hold
What matters is that I like you
And I know *that* without being told.

If Ever You Should Leave Us

When first you transferred to this school
Some people had no doubt
That what you stood for they did not
And so they transferred out
But those of us who are still here
Felt you deserved a chance
And for the most part, I must say
It was a fine romance.
Of course, ten years is a long time
And ships do get unstable
But I think most of us agree
That yes, this Kane was able
And finally when we all thought
That everything was set –
We even got to like your style
Though not your memos yet –
You let us know you might move on
You say that you might leave
So here's a poem that I wrote
That tells you how we'll grieve:

If ever you should leave us
For that job you so desire
No one will sit *shiva*
And no one will retire
In fact, if you should leave us
A party we will make
At which we won't serve celery
But lots of gooey cake
We'll say goodbye to healthy snacks
Hello to food that's junk
The kids will dress in far out clothes
Their hairdos will be punk!

If ever you should leave us
You might awake the devil
We'll get a text for every kid
And all on the same level
And if that isn't bad enough
To really seal your doom
We'll set aside an hour each day
And read around the room!

If ever you should leave us
Don't think you'll cause us pain
And don't expect to see us
Use the right side of our brain
And if a word like *hemisphere*
Is ever on a test
We will not answer *left* or *right*
But only *east* or *west*!

If ever you should leave us
We will not make a scene
We'll trade in all that SOI
For one ditto machine
And for a goodbye present
We'll give you every kit
And we will even tell you
What you can do with it!

If ever you should leave us
There won't be any fusses
We'll all give tests marked A, B, C
We might even give plusses
And as for types of questions
We'll use when you've said *bye*
We'll ask just hundreds of the *what's*
And not a single *why*!

If ever you should leave us
We'll really be okay
And we'll invite you back to school
On Graduation Day
And if ever we remember
That you didn't treat us right
We'll set that graduation
Not for daytime but for night
And the boys will wear tuxedos
And the girls will all wear jewels
And we'll hand them their diplomas
Right in front of the whole school!

But no, you'll never leave us
There's no way that you'll go
You're not the type of candidate
They want at Central O
You have a sense of humor
Your ideas are too grand
You speak your mind
You stir things up
They just want someone bland
No, you will never leave us
So this is not adieu
No, you will never leave us
Alas, we're stuck with you.

Everybody's Talking

These days at Tackan, wherever you go
You hear that morale has gotten so low
That unless we do something, unless we rally
We might have to rename our school Death Valley.
How did it happen and what has gone wrong
And why and on whom does the blame belong?
Who are the stars, the supporting cast?
How long will this terrible climate last?
Will we ever joke and talk about sex?
Is this a soap opera or Oedipus Rex?

Now the memos are longer and much more obscure
The Cabinet's meeting, will they find the cure?
The nuclear war and the Middle East
We've put on hold, for now at least
And we're all wondering while deep in our panic
If Captain Kane can save this Titanic
Or if he'll blow it by acting un-cool
And if we'll mutiny and take o'er the school.
As for a leader, we're not at a loss
Lois *already* thinks she's the boss!

But in the meantime, you can feel the tension
There are certain words that you mustn't mention:
And what is amazing and really quite strange
Such innocent words as *schedule change*
Say the words *bus duty* and you've sealed your doom
Two people will send you to an early tomb
And words like *patrol* and *lack of trust*
May lead to words like *dust to dust*
And if you think you're independent
Try saying the word *superintendent*!

Still, everyone's gabbing and everyone's squawking
And even the tactful Elaine is talking
And all that you hear in the Teachers' Room
Is who did what and when and to whom.
What some people think, though, we'll never know
Because to our rooms at 8:50 we go
And though their ideas may be divine
They don't get to school till 8:49.

So what's to be done? What action to take?
Karen seems to think all we need's a snake
And if you ask Mery, you know what you'll get
"Paint your toenails green and get on a jet!"

And who is studying and writing reports
About school morale? Why Lois, of course!
Because in three schools where she previously taught
There were similar problems and she solved the lot!

And Dianne's deciding which side of the brain
Deals with school morale and resultant pain
And she'll let us know when she finds the cure
But knowing Dianne, not so fast for sure.

And then there's advice from Judy Levine
"Just mean what you say and say what you mean"
And yes, that advice might be A-okay
If only we knew what she meant to say.

But Bill sees no problem and he sheds no tears
He hasn't had this much fun in years
And let's not ask Barry how to end this strife
Or we'll all be doing bus duty for life.

On second thought there's no need to bother
I have the solution and it's like no other
The way I propose this fire to douse
Is for Bernie to buy Barbara Stanley's house
And then for Barbara to reciprocate –
She could let Bernie keep her children late.
And the happy ending to this Tackan fable
Sees Barbara and Bernie at the same table
And Barry off his patrolling perch
And back in his office doing his research.
Then the rest of us, we could all go home
And I could stop writing this interm'nable poem!

Of Three I Sing

Our school board this year was very inventive
And offered its teachers what's called an incentive
And what that means is that it's okay
To take those teachers with the highest pay –
And even if they might be tops
Creative, kind and break their chops
To do a job that youth can't touch –
Get rid of them, they cost too much.
And what technique does the school board use?
It makes them an offer they can't refuse
Well... *almost* can't because with our three
– Elaine and Urs and Billy V –
It took soul searching of the deepest kind
Before they finally made up their mind.
Every time we'd see them, they were on their way
To another meeting of the STA
Coming back from meetings, giving us the news
How much they would gain, how much they would lose
Maximums, percentage, sick days, health insurance
A test of their knowledge and of our endurance
How long would this last? Couldn't God be kind
And help those three make up their mind?
Finally, it seemed they were on their way
But one thing they lacked – Lois's okay
So Mondays it was *yes*, Tuesdays it was *no*
Wednesdays it was *stay*, Thursdays it was *go*.
At last they announced that for sure it's *yes*
Grace broke down and cried, I bought a new dress.
And so, yes, they're leaving but ere they're retired
We do have to tell them why they're so admired
And since that task somehow fell to me
Here it is set down for posterity:

First we have Elaine serious and demure
She is so soft spoken that you're never sure
What it is she's saying, though you strain your ears
I haven't heard a word in years
But if I did, I know they'd be
Gentle words and honest and of malice free
Elaine never gossips and she never will
Not if she resisted, carpooling with Bill.
We'll miss all the costumes, all the props and such
Her part in productions where she did so much
Yes, she did a lot and with grace and poise –
A little like Lois but with much less noise –
But Elaine's not perfect, no she's not yet there
Last week she did something that's beyond repair
Walked out of her room and while she was gone
She did the unpardonable, she left the lights on
Well, she was discovered, you can guess the rest
I hear that Elaine is under arrest.
Let that be a lesson – now in education
Leaving a light burning's cause for consternation.

Then there's Ursula organized and neat
Running Student Council which is quite a feat
Collecting bottles and sometimes glass
Always speaking softly when it's to her class
Not when it's to us though, 'cause at us she'll holler
We didn't make coffee, we owe her a dollar
And she won't accept it after 12 o'clock
On and on and on, Ursula can talk
And Ursula's stories, they kind of extend
They've a start, a middle but alas no end
She began a tale one fine summer night
And eight years have passed – still no end in sight
Since she started it, two wars we have won
All the boys are home, but Urs? – Still not done.
And so, should you pass by this room some day
And should Urs be talking, better run away!

And then there is Bill. Who else stands so tall?
Serving on committees, answering every call
Funny, entertaining, making us all laugh
Second best joke teller on the whole, whole staff
But Bill has one gift at which he's sublime
And one that like wine is seasoned with time
We all know people who can do things well
Like sing or write or read or spell
Some are best at cooking, some are best at knitting
But no one can equal Bill's talent for sitting!
There is no one else, no one anywhere
Who is so at peace, at one with his *chair*
– Nolan Ryan may be king of the no-hitters
But Bill is the Laurence Olivier of sitters –
Billy and his chair, an act of communion
Since the Civil War there's been no such union!
So before you leave, Bill, we hope that you will
Maybe give a workshop on your special skill
And if it's for credit or perhaps for pay
We'll all come to watch Billy sit his way
And then maybe next year when it's Arbor Day
We'll invite you back from your holiday
To a celebration at which we'll install
A chair just for you in the Nature Mall
And if you are good and Lois don't rile
She'll put it right next to Barry's sundial.

So now they're retired, will their life be bliss?
I see it looking something like this:
Ursula and Ralph all that time together
Hours upon hours no break in the tether
Ursula and Ralph so much time somehow
Guess they'll fix the house, I can see it now –
He wants to paper, she wants to paint
He says he is, she says he ain't

He wants Virginia, she wants Vermont
He says he'll go, she says she won't
He says the mountains, she says the bay
A retirement nightmare is what I say.
What will fin'lly happen? That is not a myst'ry
Urs will buy a gun and Ralphy will be hist'ry!
Then she'll write a book called *My Life with Ralph*
All about an alien – or is that one *Alf*?
Later she'll do talk shows and in all her glory
To Phil and to Oprah she'll retell her story.

Elaine will change, she'll start to frolic
And probably become an alcoholic
And who can blame her after her hard day
Of milking the cows and mowing the hay
Carrying in water, shoveling the snow
Wondering where those damn chicks did go
Shearing the sheep, all day on her feet
Worried if the horses had enough to eat
Elaine on the farm – that should test her mettle –
I bet that she'll make a perfect Ma Kettle!

And where is our Billy? Is he okay?
Is he attending every matinee?
Soaking up culture, acting so refined
Going to the opera, improving his mind?
But wait, methinks I see Bill there
Walking in a raincoat up and down Times Square
Going to the movies but always the ones
With names such as *Lust* or *Wild Thunderbuns*
Oh, just what has happened to this poor man's brain?
Everything we taught him, all gone down the drain
I think that Bill needs tender loving care
Quick somebody, hurry, go get him his *chair*.

Okay, that's enough, now you can relax
I have put away both my knife and ax
And now is the time, time to celebrate
And tell you sincerely that we think you're great
And to say we'll miss you which is obvious too
Not for what you did but because you're you.
For so many years you three have been here
And our lives have touched and you've become dear
We have shared our sorrows, we have shared our joys
We were all connected through these girls and boys
Who passed through our hands, who were in our care
I know that they'll wish you were here not there.
Long ago we chose this work that we do
Oft the road was rough but we saw it through
'Cause we cared for kids and 'cause we still care
And that love is something that we'll always share.
So farewell to you – Urs, Elaine and Bill –
We do hope someday, if you like us still
That you'll come to call, if this way you pass
Maybe on a Wednesday – bottle day, no glass!

The Ballad of Lois, That Is
(To the tune of *The Ballad of Jed Clampett*)

Well, Lois, you've been dreaming of this day for many-a-year
I'm sure you're very happy that it finally is here
And I was just as eager for this day to come along
Because I couldn't wait to sing you this here little song –
A roasting, that is, with lots of meat.

'Cause ever since we met way back in 1984
I knew the day would come when I would even up the score
We worked together all those years, you told me what to do
But now the tables they are turned, I'm here to torture you –
Nail you, that is, watch you squirm.

The worst thing that you put us through, I finally can tell
Both Marianne and I agree were those field trips from hell
But you believed in them so much, and so what could we do?
We shot for it, the one who lost went on the bus with you –
Stuck with you, that is, for the whole day.

How many of those trips there were, thank God I've now lost count
The ones I can't forget were those to William Sidney Mount
'Twas not exactly rock-and-roll, the kids were bored to tears
And me with every trip we took, I aged like twenty years –
Dullsville, that was, sheer boredom.

Another thing that made us weep was all that science stuff
You ordered earthworms, crickets, mice, you couldn't get enough
And when they'd come, I'd lose my lunch, while you, you loved it all
But me I'm Jewish, I don't know from things that creep and crawl –
Grasshoppers, that is, chameleons, owl pellets, oy.

And when you started talking we could see no end in sight
You'd keep us there the whole day long, you'd talk into the night
You'd block all the escape routes so we really had no choice
And then your voice, it's louder ev'n than Barbara Hansen's voice –
And that is loud, that is.

And when the time to order our supplies arrived in spring
You took home every catalog and ordered everything
Our rooms were filled up to the brim with every book and toy
I'm sure you knew how much we loved your favorite, *Farmer Boy* –
Torture that was, pure suffering, 280 pages of it.

Well, Lois, I could probably go on for quite a while
But I don't want to overstay, that's really not my style
And I remember well what happened last year, what it took
When you would not get off the stage, we had to get the hook –
Drag you off, that is, talking all the way.

But ere I go I have a few things I'd like to report
Of all the people that I hit on, you were the best sport
And even though you were my foil and got more than your due
The truth is that the best things that I learned, I learned from you –
Indians, that is, I mean Native Americans, projects, reports, MST.

Well, Lois, you've already proved no task's too hard for you
And now that you will have more time, who knows what you will do?
It seems that word is spreading that you're getting all prepared
I hear that in Afghanistan Bin Laden's running scared –
Chicken that is, under a rock, go get him, Lois.

A Change of Room

That life is not easy, I'm quite aware
And everyone's given a cross to bear
And this year the cross that was placed on me
Was to be across from Room 43.

Back in September, it seemed ideal
An empty room had such quiet appeal
But I soon discovered that I was wrong
'Cause empty and still it did not stay long.

I don't know who was first, my memory fails
Either Robin's robots or Maude's Christmas Tales
But once it got started, it got really loud
The smell of the grease paint, the roar of the crowd.

One day I heard this mighty roar
I rushed to the room and opened the door
Ten kids were running, what looked like a lap
"It's part of a project we're doing for HAP!
We're supposed to run until we tire
Then check our pulse to see if it's higher."
"Hey, kids!" I tell them and I have to shout
"The answer is YES! Now please just get out!"

One time while I'm teaching my class to spell
Somebody calls out, "Hey, what is that smell?"
And while I'm not sure, I do have a hunch
I think Robin's class is in there for lunch.
They traced their roots at which they were good
So now they're sampling their ancestors' food
It's called learning by doing, which is quite the rage
But... learning to eat? At ten years of age?

And every Thursday, sharp at two
The Fifth Grade Chorus with you know who
And although I'm sure they make Bernie proud
Why do they have to sing so LOUD?

On Friday morning it comes once more
Excedrin headache one hundred four
The Fourth Grade Chorus in finest mettle
I know every word of Hansel and Gretel.
(And as I awaken each Friday morn
I curse the day Humperdinck was born!)

And what's this I see on a day in May?
It's Dorothy Lamour and she's heading this way
No, it's Barbara Stanley and she's doing her thing
I expect any moment to see Bob and Bing.

But what has got me in total panic
Is that Barbara's talking about things volcanic
It's nine in the morning and I'm already dyin'
How do you say *oy veh* in Hawaiian?

So we've had one luau and three films on sex
While my kids are straining their ears and their necks
And nothing I do can quite compare
With whatever is going on in there.

So I told my class to close the door
And not to look there anymore
But I didn't want them to feel too bad
So I said they may look out the window instead
And then to the horror of one and all
I see they're building a Nature Mall!

Now each afternoon, I'm raving and ranting
While Elaine's class is digging and Gloria's is planting
And while I am still hot under the collar
That's when our Maude decides to go solar.
And Maude will do things to the *nth* degree
She's in every space surrounding me
And while I'm sure her kids think it's fun
I am beginning to DESPISE the sun!

But what the heck, I grinned and bore it
The year is over and I'm better for it
They can do whatever they want next door
I know it won't bother me anymore.

I was ready for anything that came my way
Except what Elaine said to me today
Which assured me that, yes, I was going insane
"My room will be empty next year," said Elaine.

So here to Barry is my request
For a room – I hope he can fill –
Far from the office, far from the *john*
But a little closer to Bill.

Those Were the Days
(To the tune of same)

Here we are at your retirement party
Bidding you farewell, saying good bye
All dressed up and charming and still sober
Hoping Barbara Stanley will not cry.
We have gathered here to sing your praises
To be complimentary we'll try
So relax and let us entertain you
As we tell you tales of days gone by.

Those were the days, my friend
We thought they'd never end
Especially the ones without a break
We'd lead the life we'd choose
We'd fight and never lose
Working for you would be a piece of cake.

How well we recall your famous schedules
Schedules that were...well... what can we say?
You and June worked months and months to give us
Music, Art, and Gym on the same day.
Then we'd get to school early September
Tell you that your schedule's not sublime
So you'd start to fix it and correct it
Now we've Art and Gym at the same time.

Fondly we remember all your memos
Those pink sheets that made us all see red
I guess maybe now's the time to tell you
Yes, those memos were above our head.
Finally we did learn how to read them
Finally the hang of them we got
Finally we really understood them
Skipping each third word sure helped a lot!

Those were the days, my friend
We thought they'd never end
Especially the ones without a break
We'd lead the life we'd choose
We'd fight and never lose
Working for you would be a piece of cake.

Then there were the teacher observations
How we'd wait and worry every day
But there really was no need to panic
You would not show up till end of May.
And by that time, frankly, we were tired
Energy and eagerness we lacked
Dreaming of our summery vacations
So what you saw was how well we packed.

When you came, all sweets went out the window
You'd only allow those sugar-free
But no matter how we would promote it
No one ever asked for celery.
And of course, you put a ban on cupcakes
And on birthdays too, you made that plain
And as a result there'll be dysfunction
And it will be blamed on Barry Kane!

Those were the days, my friend
We thought they'd never end
Especially the ones without a break
We'd lead the life we'd choose
We'd fight and never lose
Working for you would be a piece of cake.

Discipline was something that concerned you
Children should behave, so what to do?
You invented that Deportment Letter
Now the mail cannot keep up with you:
"My Dear Mrs. X, let me inform you..."
It's Deportment Letter number ten
"Johnny spit a noodle at Joanna
And beat up the lunch aide once again."

"My Dear Mrs. X, I hate to tell you..."
This is notice number fifty-five
"Yesterday your Johnny chased Joanna
Stabbing her with spoons and forks and knives."
On and on these notices keep coming
"My Dear Mrs. X, we're not amused..."
And in school the discipline's not changing
But a lot more paper's being used.

Those were the days, my friend
We thought they'd never end
Especially the ones without a break
We'd lead the life we'd choose
We'd fight and never lose
Working for you would be a piece of cake.

Of the various changes that you brought us
There was one which many of us cursed
How you rearranged our grade assignments
So we'd never know who'd be in First.
But I think I know how you decided
It would not surprise me, not at all
See, one day I walked into your office
And saw a dartboard hanging on your wall.

Those were the days, my friend
We thought they'd never end
Especially the ones without a break
We'd lead the life we'd choose
We'd fight and never lose
Working for you would be a piece of cake.

Now you're going off and we're assessing
What it was you did around this place
True, you made us right-brained and holistic
But most other things were done by Grace.
Well, as you can see, we did remember
And as you can see not much we missed
And just to make sure you don't forget us
We'll end this song by singing your class list:

So good-bye from Winnie, Sheila, Janie
Lois, Lexi, Karens V and P
Dianes, Carols, Ursula and Barbaras
Molly, Sallie, Bonnie, Rosemarie
Beth, Elaine and Lisa, Nancys, Billy
John, Paul, Grace, Rose, Mery and Marie
Eileen, Ron, Pat, Doris, Lindas, Teri
Judies, Joan and June and Joyce and me.

I'm Still Here

We're gathered here in the best of schools
Where Pat is boss but Rudin rules
To celebrate those of us who
Having much better things to do
Than stand around and teach all day
Are out of here. They're on their way.
But we are wond'ring ere they go
What felled those nine with just one blow?
And if it was some strange disease
Why was it only Tackanese?
The other schools, e.g. Paul Graff's
Are they too losing half their staffs?
And if they're not, what did we do?
I'd worry, Pat, if I were you.
No, we won't rest until we know
Just what it was that made you go:
Did you find some of us too cocky?
Did you hate Netter's walkie-talkie?
Or the red ribbons and red bows?
Or was it Mery Flaherty's clothes?
The interruptions and the calls?
Was it the scuff marks in the halls?
Or Mulhall's photos on display
Of a new grandchild every day?
Was it Colleen Catrini's mouth
That made you want to head down South?
Or was it Grace's tale of woe
Her evil eye, her Uncle Joe
That made you think you flipped your lids?
Thank God she's marrying off those kids!
Enough! I'll speculate no more
Let's do what we have come here for
And so, for better or for worse
Each retiree now gets a verse.

Compared to Viv, we all look sick
She's got a deck, a dock, a Dick
Hope you and he won't fight next year
Or you might wish you were back here.

Diane forever will remain
The champion of our right brain
She is retiring 'cause of stress
From now on she'll do even less.

For Karen, just one word – unique –
Was that her mouse we just heard squeak?
Karen will move, she'll pull up stakes
And birds and cats and dogs and snakes.

And Ron, there's no doubt about you
Each one of us knows what *you'll* do
But really, golf, all night and day?
Don't you have better things to play?

And Joyce, so cultured, so refined
She loves to talk, she speaks her mind
And I'm just wond'ring come next fall
Who'll hold us captive in the hall?

And Terry's talent is to shop
Next year she'll do it without stop
Yes, she and Winnie'll have a ball
When all day long they walk the mall.

And next year Winnie, who's so bright
So well informed, so erudite
Plans to do something quite profound –
Yes, shop herself into the ground.

Lorraine, so gentle, never crude
We all admire her attitude
One reason I found her so fine
She let me cut the Xerox line.

To Sue we want to say farewell
She only stayed for a short spell
She's moving, she is not retired
And with those legs, I bet she's hired.

So, all the best, goodbye, adieu
Tackan won't be the same sans you
You were all great, above reproach –
On second thought, maybe not Coach.
You'll be replaced, of that no fear
By newer models come next year
With slender waist and firm behind –
I think that Ron just changed his mind.

And even though it may be hard
To view the changing of the guard
That's what it is. We had our day
And for the young we must make way.
So why, you wonder, don't *I* go?
It's just that I still need the dough
But soon, I too will join the throng
I promise, Jeff, it won't be long.

One of Those Years

Early in the morn, my troubles begin
Someone threw a staple into the wrong bin
And there's purple paper in the bin marked "Yella"
I'm sure I'll be hearing from Vinnie Failla.
And in the blue basket, there's – oh, no – a GRAPE!
I'm about to scream when I see the tape
And if grapes are taped, they go in the Blue –
Unless they are stapled or shows signs of glue.
No one can imagine the turmoil I'm in
Wondering all day, "Is this the right bin?"
And it's not just me, my kids too don't know
The most oft asked question is, "Where does this go?"
By three garbage cans I've become bewitched
I just cannot tell which garbage is which
It all looks the same but it cannot be
Because if it were, I'd have one, not three.

Now my room is freezing, cold air blows a storm
And just where is Ed? I'm sure somewhere warm
But he comes to check. Who knows *what* he does?
And how come he's wearing his coat, hat and gloves?
"Everything is fine," he says as I freeze
And goes back to his 85 degrees.

And what is Pat up to as the halls she roams?
Is she booking us into Nursing Homes?
Or maybe she's wondering just what it all means
Or is she dismantling those Xerox machines?

My class, they know nothing, for their lots I fear
But who's there to blame? *I* taught them last year!
There is just one thing that they're experts in –
Dropping the wrong trash into the wrong bin!

And now thanks to Mery and her new career
I have twenty earrings hanging from each ear
And she won't give up till I buy a pin
Which I'd like to chuck but don't know which bin.
What a year I've had! But on second thought
I don't really crave other people's lot
Take for instance Judy, I mean Judy C
In her worn out shoes, I'd not like to be
Tackan's homeless person, walking to and fro –
Just where is her room? Does anyone know?

And then there is Grace, Tackan is her station
This is where she stops in between vacations
But I've seen poor Grace transformed into jella
Would *you* like to work under V Failla?

And what about Viv, great figure and face
But I'd really rather not be in her place
Though I do respect her and we're real good buddies
I can do without teaching Social Studies.

Then there's poor Joyce Miller, classy and refined
If I had her class size, I would lose my mind
For Chorus one day, way too many came
Ever since that day, Joyce is not the same.

So now the year is over, another poem's done
And I am sending wishes, the best to everyone
If you would like a copy, we'll run some off for you
But when you're done, *remember* to chuck it in the Blue!

A Tackan Christmas and Hanukkah, of course

Well, here it is that time again when I'm supposed to write
And I thought that maybe this year I'd do it with no bite
But when I looked into my soul and tried to be Thoreau
A little voice inside me said, "Go back to what you know."

So I succumbed, put *grand* on hold, yes, I gave up the quest
And I decided to go back to that which I know best
I'd try again next year, I thought, for now I'm off high Art
And once again was on my way to picking folks apart.

But as I thought back on this year it was obvious, it was plain
That everyone was normal that everyone was sane
And no one was neurotic and nobody was queer
And I began to really miss the kooks of yesteryear:

Like Veit and that constrictor she wore around her neck
And Bill Vogt's ethnic humor, politic'ly incorrect
And Ursula's Ralph stories which were always in demand
And Barry Kane's pink memos that none could understand
He spoke a different language which was way above our head
And only Diane Wetjen ever knew just what he said
They had us all convinced that of knowledge they were full
But there is no denying that bull is bull is bull.

So if these walls could talk now, they'd tell you quite a tale
One year we had a Holy War and Carlsen sure got nailed
You see she brought a tree to school, a Christmas tree she had
And put it in the Teachers' Room and all the Jews got mad.

But now I'm in the present and I think of everyone
And everyone is lovely and no one's any fun
And I go back to writing and I'm trying to think *mean*
But how can one have unkind thoughts 'bout Sue or 'bout Justine?

By all the usual suspects I see I've been betrayed
But there is one without whom I cannot make the grade
The one I really count on to be grist for my mill
Has quietened and softened and filled up on goodwill
How can there be a poem and how can I be saved
When my greatest inspiration, when LOIS is behaved?
What's happened to our Lois? Does anybody know?
I miss that feisty Rudin, so yell at someone, Lo!

And even Pat has mellowed, we rarely see her frown
She lets us do our thing now as long's our chairs are down
Those chairs sure got to Pat, though, we felt the aftershocks
They warranted five memos in everybody's box.

And Jeff's become a softie though he still wears many hats
And I don't know whose job he wants, if it's Grace's or'f it's Pat's
But you can usu'lly find him in the office, so I'm told
While back there in Room 39 his kids are good as gold.

And the Special Ed Department is very hard to tease
They're always so, so serious, they're doing IEP's
And Merillie might kill me so I'd better not start up
But she is no fun either since she started covering up.

And even Mery Flaherty seems ordinary now
We've seen the mismatched shoes and socks and we've all seen her
bow
We're all immune to her attire, what's one more hat or less
So if she wants a rise from us, she might have to undress!

Perhaps I could pick up some *dirt* – some dirt that I don't know
If I would go to Happy Hour where all the lushes go
Like Grace and Jeff, the Ginas and Cheryl too, I think
From what my sources tell me, those Ginas sure can drink!

Well, with that happy image, I'll let this poem end
I hope there's someone out there who will still be my friend
But if you felt insulted and if you felt the bite
You must know that without you this vampire could not write.

To Pat and Grace and Lois, to Sue and Merillie
To Jeff and Gina Pensa, Maries both S and C
To Don, Lorraine, Phillipa and Mery Flaherty
To Sullivan and Skala and Cheryls S and B
To Joan and to Loretta, to Carols Mac and B
To Robin, Jim, Maria, Michael and Judy C
To Beth, Danielle and Jeri, to Barbaras H and D
To Marianne and Ellie, to June, Jack, Leslie B
To James, Colleen and Sheila, Eileens both C and D
To Jean. Pat Metz, Corrado, to Fran and Beverly
To Mary Jane and Hester, to Donnas V and D
To Ann, Lenea and Joseph, Elaine and Cathy C
To Eleanor and Linda, to Rose and Noreen B
The lunchroom aides and helpers, to Lexi and to me.

Goodbye to my Last Class

For Ashley, Evan, Ally
Concetta and Leeann
For Travis, Jenny, Rachel, Mikes
Both O and S and Dan
For Karalyn and Richard
Amanda, Brittany
For Trevor and for Andy
For AJ and Matt B
For Steven, Stephen, Brian
And also Anthony
For Tony and for Kara
For Robert, Laura, Bree:

Well, boys and girls, fourth grade is done
And it's been lots of fun
I'll miss you all, I liked you all
Yes, each and every one

The ones who worked, the ones who tried
And always gave their best
The ones whose projects were so great
As well as every test

The ones who liked the challenges
The math, the parts of speech
The homonyms, the antonyms
And other things I'd teach

The ones who talked and talked and talked
And still had more to say
The ones whose acting was superb
In the poems and the play

The ones who liked the books I read
The blowpops that I brought
The ones who always got along
The ones who ALWAYS fought

The ones who argued all day long
From nine o'clock till three
The ones who dropped things, fell off chairs
Just to annoy poor me

The ones who asked the strangest things
And who always complained
That they did not know what to do
Right after I'd explained

The ones who didn't care for work
But who'd much rather play
The ones who asked to leave the room
At least ten times a day!

I'll miss the stories that you wrote
I'll miss the games we played
I'll miss your jokes, they made me laugh
But not the MESS you made!

I'll miss the questions that you asked
You had so much to say
But one I'm sure I won't miss is
"Will we have math today?"

I'll miss the ones I couldn't hear
I'll miss the ones who yelled
I'll miss the tales you loved to tell
But not the way you spelled

And I'll remember Evan for his geography
Yes, he knew every capital, each one from A to Z
And he knew every country, the ones both near and far
And I'll remember Ashley for she did every *star*

And I'll remember all the things
You did that made me proud
Like when you listened and behaved
But not when you were LOUD!

I'll miss you all because you cared
Had feelings, showed concern
But what I'll miss the most of all
You *all* wanted to learn.

So, boys and girls, fourth grade is done
And you each played a part
You will live on here in this poem
As well as in my heart

And someday when I reminisce
And look back on my past
I think that I'll remember you
Because you were my last.

Goodbye Tackan

(To the tune of *You Are My Sunshine*)

We are retiring, yes, we're retiring
We've had enough so we're out the door
Goodbye to standards, goodbye to rubrics
Oh please, don't make us come here no more.

Goodbye to plan books due every Friday
If you don't have them, Pat is sore
Goodbye to lunch counts and Safety Sally
Oh please, don't make us come here no more.

Goodbye to meetings and to committees
Goodbye to getting up at four
Goodbye to Gina and all her babies
Oh please, don't make us come here no more.

Goodbye to PARP week and to red ribbons
Goodbye to DARE and STARE and DEAR
Goodbye to Lisa and all her boy friends
We've done our time so we're out of here.

Goodbye to push-ins, goodbye to pull-outs
And interruptions, we've had our fill
Goodbye to Mery and all her flavors
Of Bryer's, Edie's and Turkey Hill.

Goodbye inclusion, the latest torture
We're glad we left here before you came
Goodbye to Netter, goodbye to Hansen
Our ears will never again be the same.

But we've been coming here for so long now
That maybe teaching is all we know
And we're afraid that when we're not working
All we will do is eat and spend dough!

Will we adjust to the outside world now
And stay the course or will we stray?
And will we make it even though Lois
Will not be there to show us the way?

For sure we'll miss all our friends and colleagues
We'll miss the gossip, the latest *plot*
We'll miss the bagels, we'll miss the cream cheese
And knowing who has jobs and who not.

And to the children, the little darlings
We'd also like to say so long
We'll miss their fidgets and constant talking
And all their answers which mostly were wrong.

Yes, there's no doubt that we'll miss the children
For them we came here every fall
And even though they were only human
It will be them we'll miss most of all.

But that won't sway us and that won't stop us
Retirement's here, it's a done deal
Before we leave, though, we'd like to tell you
In simple words just how we three feel:

Nyeh, nyeh, nyeh, nyeh, nyeh, nyeh, nyeh, nyeh, nyeh,nyeh
Nyeh, nyeh, nyeh, nyeh, that's how it ends
Those were the good days, but they are done now
Goodbye to Tackan and all of our friends:

(To the tune of *Those Were The Days*)

Yes, goodbye to Pats, Jeff, Lois, Lexi
Cheryl, Robins, Carols M, B, C
Marianne, Eileen, Beth and Loretta
Judys, Bernadette and Stacey T
Sheila, Mery, Mary Jane, and Barbara
Jim, Jean, Leslie, Ginas S and P
Donnas, Jack and June, Chris, Tom and Jeri
Bev, Lorraine, Fran, Linda, Sharon P
Lisa, Sues, Michael, Noreen and Hester
Don, Elaine, Melissa, Stephanie
Eleanor, Teresa, Lori, Laura
James, Lanae, Arlene and Danielle C.

Bonni Smiles

We have gathered here this Wednesday
To pay tribute to a friend
A fine teacher and a colleague
Who was with us till the end

She was just a tiny person
But in memory stands tall
On this school she left her imprint
And she touched us one and all

Though it's sad that she's not with us
And it's sad that she is gone
In our hearts we still remember
In our hearts she still lives on

And, oh yes, we do remember
All the things she'd do and say
Full of spirit, full of magic
An adventure every day

With her field trips and her projects
Always busy, on the run
Funny Feet Day, Happy Hat Day
She made learning so much fun

With her clown face and her circus
Never running out of steam
Standing barefoot in the water
While she floated boats downstream

A collector and a pack rat
She saved all things great and small
Piled them up on shelves and counters
Till the shelves fell off the wall

So she went after the closet
And she filled it bit by bit
And when everything was in there
Could no longer open it

We remember, too, her helpers
All those mothers we still see
And it's due to their devotion
That this playground came to be

Yes, it's due to their fund raisers
That we're standing here today
And the whole world's wrapped in paper
But the kids have where to play

Since like all those who are special
Bonni saw life as a game
It's especially appropriate
That a playground bears her name

And it's sad that she's not with us
And it's sad that she is gone
But our hearts are filled with mem'ries
In our hearts she still lives on

So look closely, you might see her
Listen hard, you'll hear her call
Close your eyes and you will hear
Her footsteps coming down the hall

She is in the sky above you
In the flowers, in the trees
In the birds that chirp and chatter
In the fragrant balmy breeze

And because she loved small children
Full of antics, full of wiles
While you're swinging, sliding, climbing
Just remember – Bonni Smiles

Alexa the Great

Lexi, dear Lexi, we couldn't believe it
That you would retire and finally leave it
Quite frankly, I thought if much longer you'd wait
I'd be with St. Peter at the Pearly Gate
And would not be able to roast you in rhyme
But lucky for you, you made it in time.

So what was it, tell us, that signaled ENOUGH?
We hear that your class this year was real rough
And so, was it that that made you so cross?
Or the thought that Jeff Netter might soon be your boss?
'Cause when Jeff was a teach, I'm not sure you adored him
So you might well have thought how much worse to work *for* him.

But no? That's not it? So why did you fold?
Was it 'cause all your colleagues were twenty years old
And knew next to nothing of what you'd been through
With Doug and with Barry and Pat before Sue
With Bernie and Bill, Joyce Miller and Grace
And dozens of others that passed through this place?

And so, should we tell them? Do they want to know
What happened right here all those decades ago?
Whole language and dittoes and memos in pink
That none could decipher that sure made us think
Just what was the writer attempting to say?
But clear explanations were not his *forte*
And neither was Spelling – 'twas far from sublime
An inventive speller – ahead of his time!

And so every day to school we would trek
And every day there a new kind of *dreck*
Would come down the pike – that we had to try –
But nobody ever could tell us just why.
Philosophies came, philosophies went
We'd gladly have given them all up for Lent!
Behavioral objectives, the retrieval system
Madeleine Hunter – be thankful you missed them
Higher-ups thought change would fix up the flaws
We went through more changes than at menopause
And for every change that was in the air
Just like Forrest Gump, Lexi, you were there.

But you rose above it with your dedication
You offered your students the best education
You put in the hours, were always prepared
Devoted, hardworking, creative, you cared
You did what you could with your little bunches
While all your superiors were out doing lunches.

Well… now you're retired, a different phase
You're going to love all those movies and plays
The only philosophy that you'll need to know
Is how many times a week you should go
To breakfasts and dinners and lunches – that's big –
And still not have anyone think you're a pig.

Oh yes, one more thing, I mustn't forget
There's one kind of knowledge you quickly must get
In order to banter with friend-retirees
You'd better bone up on every disease
Because that's one topic you'll cover for sure
The symptoms, prognosis, the treatment, the cure
Of thyroid, arthritis, back pain and sore feet
And all this begins the minute we meet
And then it spills over to doctors and nurses
And here there's no expert that's better than Urs is
She's also our expert on claims and co-pay
Be sure that you call her – I'd do it today.

But seriously, Lex, it's time to close shop
And just like your school days, this poem must stop
But not our good wishes for all that is best
You came and you saw. You conquered. Now rest.

It's Over Now
(To the tune of *Enjoy Yourself*)

You work and work for years and years a teacher's life is tough
It doesn't matter what you do, it's never quite enough
To please the parents and the kids and principal you try
But now it's over, thank the Lord, it's time to say goodbye.

It's over now and time to feel alive
Retirement, wow! No getting up at five
For thirty years, just how did you survive?
It's over now! Retirement, wow! It's time to feel alive.

And we remember how it started, 1969
The school was Tackan, boss Doug J and you were in your prime
You settled in but Central Office had a different plan
And so you packed your dittoes and 'twas off to the tin can.

You weren't gone long, you soon returned, a new plan was in play
Who knew what Central Office did, 'twas called the Smithtown Way
And then you left, you went on leave, maternity would call
But Tackan had no place for you when you returned next fall.

Onto Great Hollow and sixth grade you were quite happy there
But you had something else to do, produce another heir
And so you did, you had a son and everything was fine
But someone else got your sixth grade, you lost your place in line.

So once again you packed your bags this time you paid a price
You ended up in JK's school, initials will suffice
But there were things you couldn't stand and you don't suffer fools
So yes, you left them in the dust as once more you changed schools.

It's over now and time to feel alive
Retirement, wow! No getting up at five
For thirty years, just how did you survive?
It's over now! Retirement, wow! It's time to feel alive.

Well, it's been quite a few years now since you have taken flight
Which means that Mary Cahill must be doing something right
'Cause you just wouldn't hang around to take it on the chin
But actually… is there still a school in which you haven't been?

Because you had a long career you saw much that was new
Philosophies just came and went, superintendents too
But there was just one thing they lacked, no vision, not a whit
So in the end it all turned out to be a lot of… hokum!

But that's no longer your concern, it's over, gone, passé
You'll have quite different problems now – a movie or a play?
And where to shop and what to eat, baked clams or escargot?
As far as all that standards stuff, you know where it can go!

It's over now and time to feel alive
Retirement, wow! No getting up at five
For thirty years, just how did you survive?
It's over now! Retirement, wow! It's time to feel alive.

But since retirement means free time, free time to stop and look
You'll learn the trumpet and Excel but no, you will not cook
So Alec, Eli, Alan dear, I'm sure you've had a hunch
That even though there *will* be time, there'll be no home cooked
lunch.

There's something else that you will do and we who know your yen
     Would never call you on the phone on weekends before ten
  We know that you like lots of sleep, there's just one thing we dread
     That now that you'll retired be, you'll ne'er get out of bed.

          It's over now and time to feel alive
          Retirement, wow! No getting up at five
          For thirty years, just how did you survive?
     It's over now! Retirement, wow! It's time to feel alive.

          And when it's 85 degrees and everyone is hot
  There's Myra wearing hat and gloves and scarf because she's not
       But don't you worry, Myra dear, 'cause help is on the way
  You know those flashes that you feel, well yes, they're here to stay.

     And when we need a helping hand, we know just who to call
  Because you know just the right folks, in fact you know them all
       The tinkers, tailors, Indian chiefs and therapists of sex
       Are listed – and they're graded too – in Myra's Rollodex!

  But, Myra, ere we say goodbye, there's something we must stress
  It's true you'll have more time for fun but money you'll have less
And though we know that money's something, something you love
                              well
  Just think you'll never have to fix the way those damn kids spell.

  The *your* and *you're*, the *their* and *there*, all that made you see red
   That you could not, no matter how you tried, get in their head
  And since you're gone, who will there be who's equal to the task?
   So they'll just have to go through life saying *ax* instead of *ask*.

It's over now and time to feel alive
Retirement, wow! No getting up at five
For thirty years, just how did you survive?
It's over now! Retirement, wow! It's time to feel alive.

This song has lasted far too long but now at last it's done
We trust that you enjoyed the show and had a little fun
We also hope you understood what we set out to say
That though your work's behind you now, in front lies a new day!

It's over now and time to feel alive
Retirement, wow! No getting up at five
For thirty years, just how did you survive?
It's over now! Retirement, wow! It's time to feel alive.
It's over now! Retirement, wow! It's time to feel alive.
It's over now! Retirement, wow! It's time to feel alive.

I Can But Imagine

By now everyone's settled
And the kvetching has begun:
"No fair, vacation's over
And so is all the fun."
"And what about this class I got?
There's no one with a brain!"
"And this she calls a schedule?
It's driving me insane!"
"And where are we supposed to park?"
"And where the heck is Don?"
"And where's the stuff I ordered?"
And on, and on, and on...
"And when is Rosh Hashanah?
A day off we could use
We've worked a week already
Thank heaven for the Jews!"

Well, friends, it's hard to write this
When I'm not there with you
And I can but imagine
What you are going through
But, please, don't misinterpret
At what I'm trying to get
I don't want to change places
With you – at least not yet.
However, if you're thinking
This poem's rather meek
You do have my phone number
So if you want to *leak*
You know where you can reach me
I'm really not that far
But just watch out you don't end up
In front of Kenneth Starr!

The Impossible Dream

(To the tune of *The Impossible Dream*)

To dream the impossible dream
And finally have it come true
That's just what it means to retire
And, Carol, it's happening for you

You spent the best years of your life
With kids that were... what can we say?
You chose Special Ed 'cause you liked them
To us they were mostly, *oy vey*

Yes, that was your goal and that was your quest
To be a fine teacher but now you can rest
Have time for yourself, not others to please
And especially, yes, to be free of those damn IEP's
Still we know that you always were true
To this glorious quest
And although often stressful and hard
That you gave it your best

Some doozies have passed through your hands
Just who will remain *entre nous*
We don't want the first thing on Monday
For parents to come in and sue

You organized each kid so well
Their schedules were simply sublime
All day they would wait for the moment
Alas, not a one could tell time

So fin'ly we'd tell them to go
By now all frustrated we'd got
And then they'd be back in two minutes
To get all the stuff they forgot

With many you had a success
You did, though we'll never know how
You must have because with your magic
They're all of them mainstreamed by now

And I'm sure that wherever they are
They remember your kindness and trust
You taught them so many fine lessons
Like a heading is always a must

Yes, that was your goal and that was your quest
To be a fine teacher but now you can rest
Have time for yourself, not others to please
And especially, yes, to be free of those damn IEP's
Still we know that you always were true
To this glorious quest
And although often stressful and hard
That you gave it your best

So now, we your friends say goodbye
We're certain you'll miss quite a few
No doubt, you will mostly miss Lois
For how will you know what to do?

And how 'bout that staff in Third Grade
I hear they won't give Pat a rest
So will they still all be invited
To luncheon at Central Park West?

And Jeff, always good for a laugh
And Mery whose outfits… you'll miss
But not quite enough, I assure you
To give up retirement for this

The new ones you're leaving behind
They'll carry the torch very well
They're young and they're cute and they're perky
Big deal, they don't know how to spell

But seriously, they are the ones
To whom the Ed Biz we entrust
For they are the present, the future
While we are a part of the past

But ere you feel sorry for us
And sad that we no longer teach
Just think that when school starts next autumn
We'll still be stretched out on the beach!

Yes, that was your goal and that was your quest
To be a fine teacher but now you can rest
Have time for yourself, not others to please
And especially, yes, to be free of those damn IEP's
Still we know that you always were true
To this glorious quest
And although often stressful and hard
That you gave it your best

Goodbye Mary, Hello Mary

(To the tune of *Hello Dolly*)

Well goodbye Mary
And hello Mary
It's so nice to have you with us retirees
You'll love this life, Mary
Very much, Mary
You can say and you can do exactly as you please
No more the boss pleasing
Or the kids' teasing
You won't have to do their bidding, *c'est fini!*
Kick up your heels, Mary
Life is gonna be so very
Very merry, Mary, yes siree!

You can sleep all day, Mary
Catch a play, Mary
Go to movies and museums and the pool
You'll go to Saks, Mary
You'll relax, Mary
But the one place you won't have to go's Nesconset School
You have some doubts, Mary
You say it's so scary
You might just not have enough to do, you fear
It's true you worked long
Your career it was so strong
But doing nothing, that's the best career.

Nothing to it, Mary
You can do it, Mary
And you will have us to teach you all the ropes
Work is okay, Mary
When it's necessary
Otherwise we have decided working is for dopes
Instead we'll go party
And we'll eat hearty
We'll make sure your life is filled up to the brim
So lose that frown, Mary
We wouldn't let you down, Mary
And we won't even tell you about the Gym.

It's retirement, Mary
Extraordinary
It's as glorious as a sunny day in May
It's a no tears Monday
A hot fudge sundae
It's a dreamy Nureyev – Baryshnikov ballet
Yes, it's a time for laughter
It's the sweet hereafter
It's the thing that makes our life a cabaret
So run don't walk, Mary
And join in all the fun, Mary
Close the door behind, you're on your way.

And don't look back, that part is o'er, something better lies in store
Close the door behind, you're on your way.
And don't look back, that part is o'er, something better lies in store
Close the door behind, you're on your way.

Are We Having Fun Yet?

Retirement will be such fun
Now that my working life is done
I'll read and write, take courses too
Go with my grandkids to the zoo
I'll exercise, work on my fears
Maybe I'll cook – first time in years
On my computer every day
I'll surf the web, bake a soufflé
Do all the things I dared not ere
Like fly a plane, have an affair
I'll travel far, great trips I'll choose
And with the old folks take a cruise
And every day will be brand new
I'll have so many things to do!
Hey, wait a minute, something's wrong
This list has grown much, much too long
And tougher than I ever dreamed
Retirement's not what it seemed
What I was really hoping for
Was something less, not something more
It was supposed to set me free
But now it looks like work to me
And work with no remuneration
So… may I pull my application?

PART IV Melancholy

Perfection

I guess I'm not perfect, I said. I was clear.
You said, Imperfections only make you more dear.
You always know what to say, yes you do,
So now I want to be imperfect for you.

Too Much

You're sexier than any man I know
Your eyes, your lips and farther down below
Your hands, so strong and firm but gentle too
Your words, a remedy for all things blue
Your voice, the best Sinatra and Tormé
Uttering, frankly, things they'd dare not say
Beside you every other creature pales
You're good for all and everything that ails
You're brilliant, witty, funny and more such
If you were also nice, 'twould be too much

In Search of an Answer

Since I'm no longer hurt
By things that hurt before
Does that mean I love you less
Or more?

Wanting

I wanted so to be your only one
The most desired, not the everyday
But there are things that just cannot be done
You knew not how to make me feel that way.

In case you're thinking that you could not lie
That honesty is always the best call
We differ on what's moral, you and I
I never needed truth from you at all.

Record Recovery

The champagne flowed freely
Her past it was checkered
And he made the quickest
Recovery on record

A Misunderstanding

A slight misunderstanding
The other night in our suite,
When I said, "I'd like a bite, dear,"
And you gave me something to eat.

Later

We made this date a while ago,
A birthday lunch with you
And it was something that you know
I was looking forward to,
But more important things come up
Than lunch, and when they do,
We must respond, as in this case –
Internal Revenue.
So I am understanding of
The schedule that you've got,
But you never thanked me half as much
For seeing you, as not.

Sublimation

There are times we just don't feel like talking
Some things aren't easily discussed
And that's the reason for the silence
Call it busy if you must

In my Life

Of late I've been reminiscing
Nostalgia is in the air
I remember the fumbling, the kissing
And, of course, it didn't end there.

Do you ever think of those moments?
I often get hints that it's rare
Your words never honor our romance
Perhaps they are tied up elsewhere.

For me those were moments of wonder
Not one of them do I regret
And so I want to remember,
I think you would rather forget.

A Curse

My thoughts which were always diverse
Are now just of you, it's perverse
Don't know what to do
They keep pushing through
And what's even worse, they're in verse

Memory à Deux

To have lived it was a joy so rare
That now, many years later, the memory's still there,
But you turn a cold ear to my advances,
My invitation to these memory dances.

You say you don't remember, that your memory's shot,
But how can you so easily forget what I cannot?
And so it causes me perpetual tristesse
To be on the receiving end of your forgetfulness.

Second Chance

As the years progress and there's so much less
Ahead of me than behind
I'd like you to know before I go
That I never meant to be unkind

If I could do it over now
I would have loved you differently
Exactly as you were and not
The way I wanted you to be

When Less Was More

Your words – which had the power to hypnotize –
  Of all your many talents were the prize.
They could convince or scold or make me melt,
  But they were always measured, so I felt.
  Whether for lack of time or lots to do
I often sensed your rush, your words were few,
And though your many tales would always stir
  – Because you were the greatest raconteur –
They'd often dangle there, left in mid thought,
  Saved for another time but soon forgot.
These days you talk nonstop and even more,
Oh, how I miss them now those days of yore.

But Not You

(To the tune of *Toi Jamais*)

All the others send a letter
Or a tender note or better
But not you
And they answer in a minute
For their heart is always in it
But not you

They take in each word, each rhyme
They don't say they have no time
But not you
And I know that I won't die
While they wait to hit *Reply*
But not you

E-mail, they like my E-mail
Oh, I can tell they really do
E-mail, they like my E-mail
Because they answer, but not you

And although they're sometimes busy
They are never in a tizzy
But not you
So I know I can depend on
Each one's reading what I send on
But not you

No, they have no predilection
For such cyberspace rejection
But not you
And I never felt despondence
Over E-mail correspondence
Now I do

I know this is a silly so-ong
But all the feelings in it true
And as I always did, I lo-ong
My heart to open, but not you

E-mail, they like my E-mail
Oh, I can tell they really do
E-mail, they like my E-mail
Because they answer, but not you

But Not For Me
(To the tune of *But Not For Me*)

He's buying Hazel's book
But not for me
'Bout Sartre – and autographed
But not for me
I'm left to wonder why
For me he did not buy
Could he have known that I
By then had three?

We once had a romance
It's now fini
And we were more than friends
Or so said he
Am I to understand
Had I been just a friend
At least perhaps I'd land
A book for free?

I thought he really cared
What have I missed?
I guess I wasn't on
His Christmas list
He did not think of me
While on his shopping spree
For, existentially
I don't exist.

Forever Sad

It's never easy to give something up
Forced or of our own volition
For the day always comes when we wish that we could
Somehow reverse the condition

So I gave you up and I miss you now
And really that is nothing new
But what is mysterious and ever will be
Is, I missed you when I had you too

Conundrum

He never liked her friends, she said,
Complaining about such.
I worried just the opposite,
That you'd like mine too much.

Missing

I hope you know I
Didn't mean to imply
I won't miss you when I'm on my way
'Cause I will, desperately
You've become part of me
And a part that will not wash away

She

She was lucky in love
And with each new affair
She found the ideal
A man who would care
Who'd love her forever
Whose love would not quit
She heard it, it scared her
She could not commit.

So now she's involved
With one less steadfast
He couldn't care less
She thinks it will last.

You

I wrote many poems
Addressed them to you
And you, when you read them
Believed they were true
And I had the feeling
They'd not made you glad
You thought I'd betrayed you
And maybe I had

But in my defense
I'd like to say this
I thoroughly thrilled
To your every kiss
And while it is true
We once were engaged
You weren't the only
You on my page

It's All Right With Me

I was your most exciting, you said,
But not the most beautiful you ever had.
That kind of honesty could have depressed,
But I only wanted to be your best dressed.

E-Fare

Our E-mail exchanges are truly great fun,
The ribbing can't get us upset,
I think that no matter what happens online
We give just as good as we get.
So I hope you don't mind that once in a while
My teasing may burst at the seams,
Remember, if sometimes the butt of my jokes,
You're *always* the butt of my dreams.

Imperfect

I forgive all your flaws and your vices,
  Your defects, your foibles – a host!
I know that we all are imperfect,
You're just more imperfect than most.

Remembrance of Flings Past

A title for my memoir at last,
I'm calling it *Remembrance of Flings Past.*
This is the moment you turn into gel
'Cause you'd much rather I just kiss not tell.
Well, there's no need to worry or get pissed,
You didn't make it to my *Best Of* list.

Bitchy Exchange

"D'you think you're saying something I don't already know?"
That was the question that you posed as we talked to and fro.
The answer to your query quite obviously is, "No!"
Because, of course, there's nothing you don't already know.

Different Jokes for Different Folks

You took exception to my joke,
A bit of fun I like to poke,
No one was hurt, no one was harmed
But you were, obviously, not charmed.
You laugh no more where once you did,
I should think twice before I kid.

...or open it and let them know

Some moments can be so divine –
For instance, when your lips meet mine,
Almost unreal, so it would seem –
I pinch myself, it's not a dream.

Then there are others – more like chores
Spent in the company of bores
Who talk nonstop without a break –
I pinch myself to stay awake.

The Trade

He wants your money and you can't say *no*
But he'll exchange his body for your dough
And you, a true believer in amour
It hurts you that this man is just a whore.

Those who've not minded sticking out their necks
Have said, "Don't give him money only sex"
But I say, "Skip the sex, give him the loot
And that way he won't be a prostitute."

Ours Is Better

The punch line of the joke seems to imply
That the wife must put up with her cheating guy
And so she says, "*Our* mistress is better,"
But the situation shouldn't upset her
'Cause if they divorce, it will all be hers
The stocks and bonds, the jewels and furs
The house in the Hamptons, the one with the view
The cars, the apartments and the children too
And thousands of dollars in child support –
So she need not be so quick to retort
And she need not be so intimidated
And maybe the joke needs to be updated.

We're Still Hot

A four hour erection is cause for alarm
Could it have been caused by all of my charm?
Four hours and still growing with no end in sight
This surely is not an erection lite.

Could it be that rigor mortis has set in?
Should I then notify his next of kin?
None of the above, so I'll simply wait
It probably was just something he ate.

Olé!

(To the tune *La Cumparsita*)

Tantalizing
I have no trouble recognizing
That feature which I'm idolizing
That feature that's so… appetizing
A candidate for Nobel Prizing
And in this age of minimizing
I'm thrilled to see you're not downsizing
Your member's here to stay – *Olé*!

Here we are a tango's playing
But we're not interested in swaying
We have another kind
Of game in mind
We can't delay, so
Though that tango keeps on playing
We know that we won't stay to sway
I can tell at a glance
Things are ripe for romance
No, we won't dance the night away – *Olé*!

And so with the stars above
And your member down below
How come I'm still thinking of
That damn tango? It won't go.
That tango's playing in my brain
That tango's driving me insane
That tango with its sad refrain
Won't go away – *Olé*!

Hypnotizing
I find that tango hypnotizing
Its sheer perfection, mesmerizing
Its throbbing rhythm energizing
Its melody so tantalizing
Its sexual heat so slowly rising
Whereas mere size is vaporizing
The tango's here to stay – *Olé*!

La Expectations
(To the tune of *La Cumparsita*)

Expectations
I have such prurient expectations
And prurient means my concentration
Is centered on degeneration
Lascivious thoughts and morbid craving
Are signs of deviance and depraving
And that's a no-no and here's why –
Because I'm not a guy – sigh, sigh!

A Rush to Judgment

When I saw him, I thought, "What a man!
As a lover I bet he's a 10."
I said, "Come over, we'll swoon,"
And he did, but too soon.
Guess I was wrong in my estimation,
Chalk it up to premature evaluation.

You're So Smart

(To the tune of *You're So Vain*)

It was so many years ago
When first you flashed upon the scene
While you were reading the New Yorker
We were reading Seventeen
You outclassed everyone by far
With all the things you'd seen
And all the things that you knew so impressed us
Yeah, they impressed us

'Cause you're so smart
You must know that this song is about you
You're so smart
You must know that this song is about you
Don't you? Don't you?

The authors that we liked back then
Inferior they were by far
To ones you read, sophisticates,
Like Jean Paul Sartre and De Beauvoir
And existentialist was just
A word we couldn't spell
And all the things that you knew so impressed us
Yeah, they impressed us

'Cause you're so smart
You must know that this song is about you
You're so smart
You must know that this song is about you
Don't you? Don't you?

The movies that we'd flock to see
The movies that amused us so
Were nothing like the foreign films
Of your Fellini and Truffaut
For you knew just what *great art* was
And we… what did we know?
And all the things that you did so impressed us
Yeah, they impressed us

'Cause you're so smart
You must know that this song is about you
You're so smart
You must know that this song is about you
Don't you? Don't you?

The music that you listened to
Came from La Scala and the Met
We only knew the *Hit Parade*
You knew each Beethoven Quartet
And while we sang *Good Night Irene*
You sang a *chansonette*
'Cause you knew French, you knew French and we didn't
You knew, we didn't

'Cause you're so smart
You must know that this song is about you
You're so smart
You must know that this song is about you
Don't you? Don't you?

And now you have your grammar skills
Who else is able to detect
When someone says "bilinGUal"
Their pronunciation's incorrect
But even worse is when we say
"D-EYE-sect" and not "d-ISS-ect"
All hell breaks loose if we make that mistake
Make that mistake

'Cause you're so smart
You must know that this song is about you
You're so smart
You must know that this song is about you
Don't you? Don't you?

I trust you're not offended by
This little bit of fun I bring
I just cannot resist, you know
You *must* 'cause you know everything
Your foibles are my fodder and
They're also so much fun to sing
It's all in jest, all in jest and you know it
Jest and you know it

'Cause you're so smart
You must know that this song is about you
You're so smart
You must know that this song is about you
Don't you? Don't you?

I Am Busy

(To the tune of *I Am Woman*)

I'm so busy, watch me run
Don't have time for everyone
So I won't have time for you today, I fear
I just have too much to do
And I'm meeting Liz at two
But I promise that I'll call sometime next year

Yes, I am and that's what I wanna be
And I can't stop, I've too much energy
Yes, I have, I have to do it all
I am late
I'm ever tireless
I am busy

We could meet at a café
But I'll have to bring Renée
And perhaps Francine and maybe Rita too
Be consid'rate of my plight
Too few hours day and night
I'm so busy, there's so much I wanna do

Yes, I am and that's what I wanna be
And I can't stop, I've too much energy
Yes, I have, I have to do it all
I am late
I'm ever tireless
I am busy

I don't mean to be unkind
But I hope that you won't mind
If I have to make some calls, just three or four
'Cause Pauline's in town, you know
And I have to see her, so
I can only stay with you ten minutes more

Yes, I am and that's what I wanna be
And I can't stop, I've too much energy
Yes, I have, I have to do it all
I am late
I'm ever tireless
I am busy

I'm so busy, can't you see?
No one's busy quite like me
I am living ev'ry day in such high gear
While we talk I have to eat
And do dishes – quite a feat
But on Tuesdays, it's just crazy around here!

Yes, I am and that's what I wanna be
And I can't stop, I've too much energy
Yes, I have, I have to do it all
I am late
I'm ever tireless
I am busy

I Am Silly

(To the tune of *I Am Woman*)

I am silly, have you heard
That there's nothing more absurd
Than the letters that I write, the things I say
I am silly, what I feel
Is not genuine, not real
I just strike and hurt whatever's in my way

I am silly, I am dumb
My ideas are ho-hum
I have never had a thought that's really deep
I am silly, I'm a bore
My I.Q. is minus four
Just watch out that I do not put you to sleep

Yes, I am and there's nothing I can do
And I can't forget, I'm reminded by you
That I can't, I can't do anything
I am dense
I am insensitive
I am silly

I can talk from dusk to dawn
But I'm sure I'll make you yawn
'Cause my talk is mostly silly and so trite
I'm a cipher, I'm a naught
I am prissy and I've got
Very little in my head, I'm not that bright

Not that bright and there's nothing I can do
And I can't forget, I'm reminded by you
That I can't, I can't do anything
I am dense
I am insensitive
I am silly

To All Those Who Keep Me Waiting

I washed the dishes, made the bed
I swept the floor, the cat's been fed
I baked a cake, I watched the news
I took a little two-hour snooze
I wrote a letter to a friend
I read a book from start to end
I listened to two symphonies
I pondered life's great mysteries
– Like which position is the best –
I watched the sun set in the West
And little did I realize
My life had flashed before my eyes.
Yes, time moves on, I'm getting old,
While on the phone, I'm still on hold!

Kiss, Don't Tell

I know there are things you consider a crime
That you wouldn't admit under oath
And I know that you practiced a lot in your time
And that's why you're so good at them both
Those names you have tripping on the tip of your tongue
Their purpose is only to fetter
They do not belong there, the place is all wrong
Your tongue can be used so much better

The Kiss

A lovely lunch, a sexy line
The atmosphere, the heady wine
Me hanging on your every word
And some confusing feelings stirred
And as I contemplate all this
Quite out of nowhere comes the kiss!
Then everything falls into place
So thanks for cutting to the chase.

To All the Men We Loved Before

You older men who once were of sound mind
Are showing signs of leaving brains behind
And taking up what seems to be the rage –
Pursuit of women who are half your age.

And that's okay, it's *chacun a son gout*
But ere you leave and ere we say adieu
I'd like, for what it's worth, here to discuss
How… well… yes… asinine you look to us.

The bald pate isn't hid by the toupee
The paunch can't be sucked in, it's here to stay
You look your age no matter what you do
The only one that's fooled is maybe you.

The children and the wives who in your wake
Are picking up the pieces of the break
Don't think of you as studs or Hercules
But rather more as lowlife, scum and sleaze.

So if you're trying to relive your youth
– Because just maybe you can't stand the truth –
At the expense of those whom you have hurt
Remember, we all get our just desert.

Yes, your day will come too, those younger ones
Will soon be hankering for firmer buns
And, though I'm sorry to be so direct,
I bet they leave you for ones more erect.

Reviewing the Situation
(To the tune of *Reviewing the Situation*)

A girl oughta have some spunk, oughtn't she?
To try an occasional hunk, oughtn't she?
And though I'd be the first to agree that on me there's no taint
I'm finding it hard to be really as square as they paint.

So I'm reviewing the situation
Guess I'm tired of being such a faithful wife
I want to sample some exultation
I think I need to try the mistress life
Get a lover who'd be good for me
And always in the mood for me
He'd never inspiration lack
And tear the clothes right off my back
He'd keep me up each night past three
Of sleep deprived I'd always be…
I think I'd better think it out again!

A real athletic younger he?
Too energetic? Just may be
And although who would want to begin an affair with a dud?
At my age do I need an Adonis who's also a stud?

So I'm reviewing the situation
And I'm thinking, young could mean an empty head
'Cause there's no greater disconsolation
Than a man who's good but only good in bed
And so while admiring his physique
I'll have to teach him how to speak
Or if I land that younger guy
Who knows what games he'll want to try?
And what if to keep up with him
I'll have to go and join a gym…
I think I'll have to think it out again!

The worst scenario I can see
He goes and falls in love with me
And he wants nothing less, so a marriage he's starting to plan
But I already have that with someone who's ten times the man.

So I'm reviewing the situation
An affair could have been simple and so nice
But in the face of this adoration
I'm gonna have to tell him it's no dice
'Cause he wants all that *forever* stuff
I say a quickie's long enough
And I want nothing but a fling
He wants to give me everything
I wanted passion – that was it
But now he wants me to commit
Until I do, he will not rest
I see he's gonna be a pest…
I think I'd better think it out again!

So what should my conclusion be?
The mistress life is not for me?
I'm a wife and have been all these years and a wife I will stay
Because roots are much better than wings, are they not, anyway?

So I'm reviewing the situation
Only wives can get to do all that fun stuff
You will be seeing no assignation
I'll continue 'cause I just can't get enough
And I'll cook for him and bake for him
Allowances I'll make for him
I'll clean for him and sew for him
That extra mile I'll go for him
I'll satisfy his every whim
And garbage I will take from him
I'll have to hear his tales of woe
I'll want to tell him where to go…
I think I'd better think it out again!

Alone

Our bond was mysterious, our hearts were connected
The pleasures were many in which I delected
But I wanted more and thought there could be
Some way to explain this strange mystery

I wanted your words to calm my unrest
But you held your tongue, your thoughts unexpressed
You said you could not, 'twas too hard for you
I thought there was nothing that gods couldn't do

I no longer ask, I don't need to know
And all this took place some light years ago
But I wonder still, when my thoughts that way flow
Why you could not give, why I craved it so

Lust to Dust

If I were younger by maybe thirty
I'd give you a photo of myself, a flirty
Rendition of me, lit up from below
'Cause once I was quite a dish, you know
And since I am me and since you are you
That snap would elicit a fancy or two.

But now I am old and Time doesn't bluff
So instead of that photo of me in the buff
I give you this token, a different reminder
Of me, and the fact that Time's always kinder
To objects like these which don't turn to dust
As surely will happen to objects of lust.

A Reflection on Caring

When we started this fling
My praises you'd sing
And shower me with compliments galore
I'd bask in the glow
That your words would bestow
When you liked how I looked, what I wore

But now it's not there
The cupboard is bare
I no longer see that raised brow
Where once you'd have panted
You now take for granted
It's like I am family now

The Fall of 1986

The fall of nineteen eighty-six
A time of new sensations
Of deep discussions, meanings deep
And deeper penetrations
The place was here, the time was now
And everything was fair
The couturiers let down their hems
And I let down my hair
The nights were soft, the days were mild
And there were mornings too
The Montauk sun, the Bay Shore moon
They smiled on me and you.

The fall of nineteen eighty-six
Six words can make me cry
Because of all the happiness
They bring to my mind's eye
The fall of nineteen eighty-six
Six words can make me wince
At what I put in motion then
At what I have done since.

Long 'fore the fall of '86
We'd talk, do you recall?
But never once did we suspect
I'd be the one to fall.

Nothing Much

A disappointment of sorts
A misunderstanding, a snit
Which I no longer recall
So how important was it?

But then I was gathering hurts
And looking for woe as I rolled
The scar tissue hadn't yet formed
My heart was still out in the cold.

So how am I now's what you ask,
Well, hardened, and heartened by such,
As well as can be expected,
I just don't expect all that much.

Melancholy Love

My love, my love, my melancholy love
Just what is this thing that I'm feeling
That brings me so close to the edge of my tears
That my heart finds so strangely appealing?

In love with my sadness, is that what it is –
Attracted to bittersweet sorrow?
Or is it more likely that time's closing in –
More yesterdays, fewer tomorrows?
Will I never do all the things I had planned,
All the things that I haven't done yet,
As well as the ones of which I'm not proud,
The ones I would rather forget?

Yet when it is over and all's said and done,
If some lucid moments I have,
I know it won't matter what I'd done or not done
But only that you were my love.

Anniversary

It happened twenty years ago today,
And what's an anniversary if not this?
And though it would be long before we'd stray,
I think about that day and our first kiss.
July the first, mimosa was in bloom,
A hot and sunny, perfect summer day,
We lunched alone in that cool spacious room,
You fed me tales along with the paté.
And I have written of that day before,
About the kiss and what it meant to me,
How it gave birth to so much, so much more,
Still in my heart, where it will always be.
I'm older now and many things have died,
But our first kiss forever will abide.

Seeds of a Dilemma

July first, 1981
First time, first lunch, first kiss
And in that lovely country inn
Were sown the seeds of this.

You claim – and I don't disagree –
That it was I somehow
Pursued, *persuaded* is your word
And that's why we're here now.

How do we see things? As they are
Or as we wish they'd be?
So on that day so long ago
You were seducing me.

A Very Good Year

It Was A Very Good Year,
Angel Eyes,
We Were Strangers in the Night
Taking a Chance on Love
And Stars Fell on…
New York, New York
In the Wee Small Hours of the Morning.
It Was a Very Good Year!

It Was a Very Good Year,
Days of Wine and Roses and Witchcraft
And Makin' Whoopee,
You Flew Me to the Moon,
You Brought a New Kind of Love to Me,
You Made Me Feel So Young,
Angel Eyes.
It Was a Very Good Year!

Love,
The thing that all men prize!
How could we realize
That love would find us
That love would find us
And it would bind us
Forevermore?
Love me and let me capture
The tender rapture
I've waited for.
More than romance would seem,
More than I dared to dream.
(Schreier-Bottero-Wayne-Jay)

More Than

(To the tune of *More Than love*)

More Than Love, a song that I once knew
Long ago, long before there was you
The sun shone down, there were no clouds, the skies were blue
And everything was still so new
When all was more than love

More Than Love, that song that Cugat plays
More Than Love recalls those other days
Heady days and starry nights on the South Shore
When we were more, oh so much more
When we were more than friends

More than friends, the song that we were fated
To play out when my heart you invaded
My defenses were all down, I couldn't win
Not from the day I let you in
When we were more than friends

Now it's late and soon time to depart
Once more, love, I'll say what's in my heart
One that's filled with joy and happiness and bliss
And which remembers every kiss
And even more than this

Fever

It was anything but halcyon
The heyday of our love
It was turmoil, it was frenzy
It was lightning from above
It was wishing, it was longing
It was passion and desire
It was momentary madness
It was hearts that were on fire
It was clawing, it was tearing
It was scaling towering heights
It was thunder o'er the ocean
It was stormy savage nights
It was poetry at midnight
It was ecstasy in pain
It was you and I in autumn
It will never be again

Lingering Sweetness

The things we ask for sometimes come to pass,
The wishes that we make sometimes come true,
And I was once a member of that lucky class,
    The first time ever I laid eyes on you.
Whoever said, "Don't wish too hard because
You just might get your wish," knew not desire.
There comes a time we step on all the laws
    As happily we jump into the fire.
And happily, oh happily I went,
For some rush in where others fear to tread,
And I loved every moment that I spent
    Doing that dreamy dance that no one led.
I'd have done anything at that time for your touch,
'Twould be the last time I'd want anything that much.

When Wavering Stops

Once I was crazy about him
He could do anything
Then I was hurt by him and didn't want to be
I wanted to tell him
I didn't want to tell him
I didn't tell him
Once I didn't want to care but I cared
Then I didn't care and was sad I no longer did.
"Do you believe that the world is round?" asked the principal
"Personally I do but I could teach it either way," replied the teacher.
Once I believed the world was round
Now I could teach it either way.

Frame-Freeze

Why more poems on this topic when there's nothing left to say –
Nothing that is not myopic, nothing that is not cliché?
All the words have been exhausted, it's the last act of the play
And we both know that we lost it, only not who walked away.

Logical Conclusion

"We're not in Kansas anymore,"
I said one day and closed the door
The outside world faded from view
And there was just the room and you.

I'd never been so far from home
Terrain was strange, the landmarks new
But I, a curious traveler,
Took it all in because of you.

And up we soared to heights sublime
On passion's wing and I held tight
Yet I was never quite as free
As there with you into the night.

The room stands empty once again
Or maybe others now explore
The lovers' bliss that once was ours
That isn't ours anymore.

The death was painless, it was quick
Still, now and then a tear will fall
But I don't cry because it hurts
A death demands it. That is all.

Looking Back

I look back at those breathless, heady days
Of endless summer, wine and roses too
When after many detours and delays
We did what we both knew that we would do.
I loosed the ribbon and let down my hair,
The sun shone brighter than ever before,
I'd come to meet you and once over there
Our need, our want could be contained no more.
I think I knew it from the very start
That of the two of us, it would be I
Who'd have a harder time if we should part,
Who'd have more heartache and more tears to cry.
For it can't last, such hunger and such thirst,
But who'd have guessed that I would lose them first?

That's Amore

Some things in life we think we won't live through
You thought my fate was such if I lost you.
You'd never have predicted this – and yet –
I have begun already to forget.

You Always Hurt the One You Love

I sense a lack of energy –
You have no will to fight with me
Insult and hurt and nail me
So how could you so fail me?

I miss my dose of cruel
When you act like such a jewel
If everything's in clover
Is S and M then over?

So bring back your satanic
Forget the messianic
I miss all that uptightness
So down with the politeness!

You've got to leave me somewhat sore
Or I'll think you don't love me anymore.

An Old Lover

Pleasant, nice and *sentimental*
Those are the words that now fall from his lips
Words not exactly transcendental
Just where is *passion, abandonment, whips?*

Love's Limit

She told you she loved you but said if she found
That you'd been unfaithful and fooling around,
She'd slash you and slice you and maim you and such –
Nobody ever loved *me* that much.

Changing Him

Trying to change him to be what you want
Is a futile attempt, I have found:
If only he talked a bit more than he does
He'd be so much more fun to be 'round
If only he thought a bit more than he talked
You'd love him forever, you're sure
And if only his thoughts were a bit less mundane
You're certain your love would endure
If only he always did what you asked
If only he'd dress with more style
If only he'd spend all his free time with you
If only he'd leave for a while
If only he thought you were cuter than he
If only he thought you more clever
If only he thought you were right and he wrong
You know you'd be happy forever.
But once the "if only's" begin to pile up
There are only two things you can do
Try changing yourself, a difficult task,
Or him – for somebody new.

We Meet By Chance...

We meet by chance and kiss hello
My mind goes back to long ago
When kisses were much more than this
When kisses held such promises

But as we talk it's clear to see
This isn't what it used to be
It's sweet but when the magic's gone
What is the sense in holding on?

There's nothing happening tonight
This isn't more than friendship lite

Waltz in no Time
(To the tune of *Waltz at Maxim's*)

He's engaged tonight
We can't meet tonight
On the go, too much snow, he'll be beat tonight
He's so busy
It makes him dizzy
No, he's not thinking of me

He's so rushed tonight
He's so pressed tonight
He'll be wining and dining the best tonight
In a hurry
In a flurry
Oh, he's not thinking of me

Mary Lou's in town
He'll see her at eight
But he can't sit down
Adeline is at nine and he's late

He must run tonight
He's a blur tonight
In a froth, he'll meet Roth, fame's the spur tonight
He's so frantic
Transatlantic
That it fills me with ennui
Oh, he's quivering with haste
Oh, he's shivering with haste
Oh, he's not thinking of me

Someone has set him on fire
Is it Jean or Phillipe or Louis?
Who's raising his temp'rature higher?
Oh, he's hot but it's not due to me

Here I am tonight
In his arms tonight
This one's caring and sharing his charms tonight
He undresses
He caresses
And he knows just what to do
He's sublime oo la la
He has time oo la la
Oh, I'm not thinking of you!

Etude for Lovers

After five years on the road
I'm bringing it all back home
We said good bye today
And I'm sitting here alone
Those tears my eyes have shed
They've cleared my head somehow
Oh, I took so long to see
But I see it clearly now.

There was a time, I thought
I would die without my fill
But this I learned from you
That things like that don't kill
And the pain I loved so much
I am throwing in the sea
I dedicate it to
The ones who'll follow me.

Still, should we meet someday
At an orgy, quite by chance
I hope you say *hello*
And ask me for a dance
Then naked in your arms
I'll relive the ecstasy
Of the times when we made love
Of the times no more to be.

Meditation in a Minor Key

So many days and months and years have passed,
Delights and joys and pleasures unsurpassed,
Exchanges which will never be forgot,
Oh, there's no doubt there once was Camelot.
And I will always think of and be glad
And cherish everything that we once had.
But lately there's been something of a strain
Which lack of time and busy don't explain,
It's more a lack of interest that I see –
A lack of interest when it comes to me.
But even that's not meant as a complaint,
It's just a statement of the way things ain't,
And neither is it really an appeal,
I'd never want to change the way you feel.
But what's become apparent over time,
I'm not your have-to-have and you're not mine.

Silence

You were there and we talked, it was not a big deal
But now that we don't, how different I feel,
I miss what I lost and what can't be returned,
Silence speaks louder than words, I have learned.

It was I walked away, quit the game, quit it cold,
I was young, I was rash, I was reckless and bold,
It was only much later that this new thought occurred –
That you, in your silence, had had the last word.

On Forgiveness

I could forgive you anything, I said, and it was true,
But that was when I loved you and I no longer do.

Breaking Up

You cannot give me what I want
And I don't want what you can give
The past was wonderful but now
This is a better way to live

I cannot give you what you want
You do not want what I can give
But that's no reason to forget
And there is nothing to forgive

Departure

A love has died, it's gone, it's lost,
You'll never be the same again,
And all those other nights you tossed
Were nothing like this present pain.
You look for solace everywhere
While trying to get through each day,
But some words are too hard to bear –
You'll find another soon, they say.
And though they don't mean to be cruel,
Words such as those no comfort bring,
They only show themselves a fool,
Who think they're saying anything.
It's just as if, of child bereft,
A mother's told, *You've still one left.*

Innocence Revisited

(To the tune of *The Only Couple on the Floor*)

The year was 1978,
We four were on a double date,
And Leda was your flame du jour,
And in the air there was *amour*.
But I was so shy and innocent back then, I was,
The real me I found so hard to expose.
Yes

It was the swinging seventies,
There was no thought yet of disease,
Free love and sex were in the air,
And everyone wanted their share.
But I was so shy and innocent back then, I was,
The real me I found so hard to expose.

You chose a lovely place to dine,
The talk was good, so was the wine,
We feasted on that Thai cuisine,
And likely scrutinized the scene.
But I was so shy and innocent back then, I was,
The real me I found so hard to expose.

A little flirting, some Merlot,
All of it to our head did go,
Where we would end up, no one knew
Before our evening was through.
But I was so shy and innocent back then, I was,
The real me I found so hard to expose.

Then like a bolt out of the blue.
It came from – well, who else, but – you,
I nearly choked on my Thai meat
When you proposed Plato's Retreat!
For I was so shy and innocent back then, I was,
The real me I found so hard to expose.

Yes, all this happened long ago,
And, well, of course, we didn't go,
And now I wonder when time lets,
Should I be glad or have regrets?

That I was so shy and innocent back then, I was,
The real me I found so hard to expose.
Yes, I was so shy and innocent back then, I was,
The real me I found so hard to expose.

The Longing

The longing was always the most painful part
'Twas there from the moment I opened my heart
And you, though you took it, the longing would stay
I never could shake it or give it away

Now all that is over, it's all in the past
Although every now and then you will ask
But if I agreed, I'd have to pretend
That what lies between us is more than the end

The truth is quite plain, there'll be no new dawn
For the longing, the longing, the longing is gone

Rondeau Redoublé

I want to write a poem just for you
I want to tell you what you mean to me
So many years have passed but it's still true
There's nowhere else that I would rather be

I do not yearn for Rome or gay Paree
I do not want to visit Timbuctu
Let others cross the ocean, sail the sea
I want to write a poem just for you

For you were there with me when it was new
You opened up my heart, you had the key
And after all these years it's still us two
I want to tell you what you mean to me

Your strength, your goodness, your integrity
Your optimism which no one can outdo
You were at once committed yet still free
So many years have passed and it's still true

So if we leave our home to start anew
It really makes no difference where we
End up, 'cause if you're there and I'm there too
There's nowhere else that I would rather be

Companion, soul mate, lover, bel ami
The years were good to us but how they flew
And now this rondeau redoublé's fini
Yet there is so much more I want to do
I want to write…

Damned If You Do and Damned If You Don't

I'd like to very much see it your way
I don't though, but that's something I can't say
I cannot tell you what is on my mind
I know that you'd consider it unkind
And you'd get angry or annoyed at best
It might just put our friendship to the test
And I don't want that, for your anger I recall
Does friendship, then, make cowards of us all?
Since I'm a friend, should I not make you see
You might be wrong? But that's the irony
I cannot tell you – and I doubt I will –
'Cause friendship too demands that I be still

You Never Told Me

You never told me if you did or not,
I never asked for you looked down on such,
At one time you were everything I sought,
I carry still the imprint of your touch.

And then one day you simply disappeared
Without a trace, a letter or a call,
It's said each man destroys the thing he loves,
If so, I guess you loved me after all.

That Moment

A moment that happened between us
That caused me such sorrow and pain
For which in the end I must blame you
Comes back and it haunts me again

Indifferent, neglectful and careless
Worse yet, you had no clue you'd erred
But I couldn't shake off that moment
When sadly I saw what you were

I should have cried out at such treatment
And forced you to look and to see
But I just continued to love you
So what does that say about me?

Melting Point

A while ago I said, no more
I'm shivering now outside your door
Guilt kept me from the Inn of Sin
But flesh is weak, may I come in?
How can I ever be absolved
If your heat keeps melting my resolve?

I'm Guilty of the Things that I have Wrought
(Villanelle)

I'm guilty of the things that I have wrought
Which bring me so much joy and yet such pain,
I wish I could let go, but I cannot.

When first we started on this journey fraught
With danger on all sides, I was insane,
I'm guilty of the things that I have wrought.

I could do anything was what I thought,
And so I did and thus I forged the chain,
I wish I could let go, but I cannot

Forget the million pleasures that you brought,
They're so much part of me, 'twould be in vain,
I'm guilty of the things that I have wrought.

But I blame no one, no, this is my lot,
Still, how I long for solitude again,
I wish I could let go, but I cannot.

If I'm enslaved, for in your cage I'm caught,
Let me at least sing freely this refrain –
I'm guilty of the things that I have wrought,
I wish I could let go but I cannot.

ADDENDUM

My Other Life

I was born on January 17, 1937 in the city of Krakow in Poland. As a child I lived there with my parents in a lovely apartment, which was possible because my mother's family was quite well to do. When I was born, my mother was 33 and my father was 35. My father was born in May of 1902 and my mother in March of 1904. I was the first child born to my parents and I am an only child but in 1939, my mother gave birth to a stillborn baby girl. I don't know all the details of that story and before my mother and I could have a heart-to-heart about the episode, she contracted Alzheimer's disease. She was hospitalized for the last ten years of her life. What I *do* know, because my mother spoke about it, was that at some time in the year 1939, in a hospital in Krakow, she gave birth to a baby girl that was stillborn. I remember her telling me that in the hospital where she was giving birth, she was made to sit or lie over some kind of porcelain vessel and that it broke under her while she was delivering the baby. I don't know if I was supposed to understand from this that this was what caused the still birth. I can't say that my mother explicitly said it. There were hints though of another cause. Again I don't remember if my mother actually voiced these – but if not, why would I be remembering it this way? Obviously, there is much uncertainty. Still, I believe that she may well have done something during her pregnancy to bring about that result. You see, to have a newborn in 1939 in Poland was surely a death sentence. So I guess you can say that that baby girl, the sister I never had, was the first sacrifice, the first Holocaust victim of our immediate family. But I'm sure that at the time it was seen as something of a blessing because had that baby survived, surely we would not have. Yet, survive we did – all three of us, my mother, father and I – quite miraculously for that time and that place. And to impress upon you how miraculous the survival of all three of us was, let me just say that out of my mother's whole family which included seven sisters and two brothers and her parents, and my father's which consisted of three sisters and two brothers and their parents, all of them married except for one and all of them with children, my parents and I were the only ones who survived the war in Poland. Two of my mother's sisters, one brother and their mother had gone to Palestine before the war and they remained there, and one nephew of my father's survived in England. Other than that, we were the only ones. At least twenty-two members of my family of aunts, uncles and first cousins perished in the Holocaust, and that's not counting my father's parents because I don't know how or when they died. It's another one of those questions that I wish I had the answer to, that I wish I had asked.

So, I was born into a fairly wealthy family. My mother's father owned a silverworks factory in Krakow where beautiful silver objects were made. He was a successful businessman as well as an Orthodox Jew, learned in the Talmud and the Torah. When my father married my mother, he went into the business as well. My parents were not as religious as their parents had been and I don't know how they observed Judaism in their home in Krakow. I'm quite sure my mother lit candles every Friday night which is a Jewish tradition. I don't remember whether she continued doing that after the war. I think she did for a while but then stopped. I remember her telling me that somewhere along the way she had lost her faith. I didn't wonder why. But I never remember my mother having been bitter or vengeful. Sometimes she would cry out at the terrible loss to her and to humanity in general brought about by the Holocaust, and the death of specific members of her family haunted her – two of her nieces in particular which I understood to have been her favorites. But she did not obsess. She was a true survivor and one of the best-adjusted people I ever knew. There was never a doubt in my father's or my mind that it was she, with her stubborn persistence and unwavering resolve, who saw us through the war. She believed that there was nothing that she could not do and she was that way all her life.

Krakow was quite large and fairly cosmopolitan unlike the small towns and rural villages where many of the Polish Jews lived before the war. I was of course too small – only two when the war broke out – to remember from first-hand knowledge. I'm sure there was anti-Semitism in Poland, in Krakow. Much about that has been written and discussed but I must say that my personal experience and that of my parents was quite the opposite. The people with whom we were in direct contact during the war were anything but. First of all there were the three families who hid us – my mother, father and I were rescued by three different families in three different homes – and to whom we owe our lives. Then there were the workers in my grandfather's factory, all Gentiles, who played a crucial part in our survival. They found the three families who actually knew each other – two of them were related and lived on the same street as my grandfather's factory was located. During the war, one of these workers accompanied my mother to the site where her father had buried some gold coins – Krugerands they were called – which were essential to our survival. Later on, this man would go there by himself and bring my mother the money. Every time he did this, he risked his life and it would have been very easy for him to have absconded with the money. There was no law to which we could appeal and if there had been, it would surely not have been on our side. It seems that my grandfather was a kind and generous boss and that may be why those who worked for him were eager to help us.

I went into hiding in March of 1942 when I was 5 and stayed hidden until January of 1945 when I was 8 and when Krakow was liberated by the Russians. The family that hid me was made up of four women and a little girl my age, named Gabi. It was in Gabi's mother's care that I was placed. The other women in the household were her two unmarried sisters and her mother. Gabi's father was a soldier in the Polish army and when I came to live with them, he had already been sent to the front. One of the reasons her mother gave for becoming a rescuer was that she thought one day, somewhere, someone might help save her husband the way she was planning to save me. Unfortunately that day never came. Gabi's father was killed in Katyn in what was for the longest time believed to have been a German massacre but which, it was discovered not too long ago, was actually committed by the Russians.

I must tell you at the outset of this part of my story that the three years I spent in hiding are very hazy, very blurry. It's as though a cloud had formed over that part of my life, eclipsing it from myself. I used to think that that was because no one could remember what happened to them at such a young age until I began talking to people who could. What I'm trying to say is that a lot of what happened to me at that time

I must have blocked out. Maybe behind that cloud are experiences which I cannot allow myself to see, which I must keep from myself. Some things I do remember. Some things were told to me by my parents and still others I learned when after 50 years of separation, I was reunited with Gabi.

The family that hid me was a very decent, hard-working one. They were observant Catholics and I remember going with them to church. I was "passing" as Gabi's Gentile cousin, and if anyone asked, I had come to live with my aunt as my own mother had taken ill. What I knew about my own religion and identity, or how my parents had prepared me for this pretense, I do not remember. But I knew that this was not a "pretend game". This was serious business. Since I did not look Jewish, whatever that means, I did not actually have to be hidden all the time and I was able to go outside. Sometimes I even went on small trips to the country to a farm owned by the relatives of the family that hid me. At times, I had to hide within the house when someone came to visit who might pose a threat or ask too many questions. I remember one instance during one of these visits when I was hiding under a sofa in the living room, in the very place the company was sitting. The furniture in the house was old and infested with lice as my new family had very little money. I remember having to lie there silently until the company left – not daring to move, call out or God forbid cough or even scratch those unbearably itchy spots. To have done so could have brought down the whole family as well as me. I was very young but even at that young age I must have understood the danger. And that was not as bad as the times when the German Gestapo came to call. They would often do house searches, sudden, unannounced and terrifying "actions", as they were called, in which they were looking for anything or anyone suspicious, in other words someone like me. If there was no time to hide, I would jump onto the lap of Gabi's mother, pretending to be asleep while Gabi played nearby. One time I hid right outside a window of the apartment which was on the ground floor, waiting there until the search was over. Had one of the Gestapo looked out that window and seen me there, more than the search would have been over. These were terrifying moments for all concerned because everyone knew what would happen, not only to me but to the whole family and maybe even all the tenants living in that building, if my real identity and true religion were discovered. Was I scared? How could I not have been? But time erases everything and feelings die. Today, I cannot recall the feeling of that fear. I do remember, however, understanding that I had to be quiet, that I had to do as I was told, that I had to control myself at all times and I think that I was smart enough, maybe wise enough to know what would happen if I didn't.

When I was reunited with Gabi in 1994, she impressed on me how attached to her mother I had become, how I followed her around and would not leave her side. I don't remember it but I believe it. Having lost one mother at such a young age, I probably couldn't bear the thought of losing another.

The story of my early education is fascinating to me. I never went to school in Poland and didn't start attending one until we moved to Paris after the war – sometime in 1946 when I was nearly 10 years old. The schools in Krakow were all Catholic, and not only was I not, but I wasn't legal and really didn't "exist". Gabi's aunts undertook my education and I learned how to read and write fluently in Polish, something which I can still do but not as well as I once did. I remember practicing my handwriting the way Gabi's aunts taught me to do it, starting by breaking each letter into lines and circles and then copying these over and over into my notebooks. The first book I actually remember reading was one I didn't read until after the war, but after that I became an avid reader and reading is still among my favorite pastimes. To this day I remember the title and author of that book, *The Heart* written by *(Edmondo De) Amicis*, but I have no memory of what it was about, though I do recall the circumstances of that first reading experience. I was bed-ridden because I had come down with the measles very soon after returning home to our former apartment which had been used during the occupation by a German officer who had left it intact.

Krakow was liberated on my eighth birthday – January 17, 1945 – and my parents came to take me home. I do not remember what surely must have been a very emotional occasion. Did my parents talk about it later? I do not recall that either but from Gabi I learned that her mother suffered the loss deeply. In the three years that I had spent in her home, she too had become attached.

I should probably interject here that during the years I was in hiding, I did see my parents – my father rarely, my mother more often. She was rather bold and took many risks in order to be able to see me. I say "risks" because all the Jews in Krakow had by this time been herded into the ghetto – except for the ones like us who were hiding illegally – and were not permitted to leave it without wearing their armband. Even with the armband, of course, no Jew was safe. In fact, quite the opposite was true. The Jewish star on the armband, this scarlet letter, so to speak, rather than protect its wearer signaled to passersby that the wearer was fair game for every insult, indignity and abuse. My mother did not wear her armband but of course that did not assure her safety. Her features were not as Aryan as mine and she could easily have been stopped on the street, questioned, uncovered and killed. Jews had no recourse. Still, my mother took that risk. I learned from Gabi that she would come once a week, probably on Sunday, and take us to our old apartment which was now occupied by that German officer with whom she had somehow developed a friendly relationship. He didn't use it on Sundays and made it accessible to her. There she would give us our weekly bath, a luxury we did not have at Gabi's house.

My mother did something else at this time which was also important to our survival. She knew how to sew, knit and crochet and she was excellent at it. She was also creative, imaginative and had wonderful taste. She would sew us these identical outfits – exquisite little dresses and aprons, beautifully embroidered and perfectly fitted. In them we were the envy and admiration of all. My mother wanted to do this and was very proud of her work and I'm amazed and in awe of her that in a time of such turmoil, tragedy and danger, she could concentrate and accomplish something beautiful. When Gabi came to visit in 1994, she brought three pictures of us taken during the war. I had never seen these pictures, didn't even know they existed. The outfits we are wearing were made by my mother. I don't know where she got the material and other accessories for these creations but one story has it that in our old apartment we had beautiful curtains and draperies. She took these down and out of that fabric made us our outfits and probably some for the other members of the household where I was hiding as well as where she and my father were. This was not only a generous thing to do but a very smart one. These favors were appreciated by our rescuers. My mother must have known that if she gave them something they liked, something they had gotten used to and come to expect, they would have had a harder time giving us up if the burden and the secret became too difficult to bear. And I don't mean giving us up to the Germans. There was no question of that. Their lives were as much on the line as ours were, but they might have had a harder time ending the unwritten contract they had made with my parents of keeping us hidden in their homes. That they could have done at any time. Of course my parents were giving them money – how much I never knew – but those Krugerands were somehow converted into Polish currency which helped to support all of us. Another reason my mother sewed, I'm convinced, especially when it came to the family that was hiding me, was that she hoped her kindness would be repaid by theirs and it was. Close to the end of the war, when the Krugerands ran out, their kindness didn't, and even though my parents had no money left to give them, they kept us in their homes until the war ended.

So, when the war was over, we returned to our own apartment which the German officer had left exactly as my mother had given it to him. The Russian armies were marching through Krakow and the mood was one of jubilation. The devastation and havoc that had been wreaked had not sunk in yet and the millions of dead had not yet been counted. The Russian soldiers, many on horseback, needed places to stay and my parents offered them part of our apartment. I don't know how many of them stayed in our house. My parents wanted to accommodate them and a little discomfort for us meant nothing after what we had been through, but I think even my parents were surprised when one day a horse appeared in our living room and our beautiful furniture had been chopped up and used for firewood. I think my parents realized it was time to leave the country.

The plan was to go to Palestine where my mother had two sisters, a brother and their families whereas we had no close relatives in Poland who had survived the war. They had all died either in concentration camps or in the ghettos or in the "actions". It was during those terrible "actions", in fact, that my mother's father, her sister, brother-in-law and those two favorite nieces and one nephew had perished. It happened in a small town where they were living, not far from Krakow. They were taken out and shot. My parents and I happened to be there at that time too but miraculously we found a shelter in which to hide and so we were spared.

We did not want to stay in Poland any longer than we had to and so while the arrangements to go to Palestine were being made, we went to Paris, France where we lived from 1946 to 1949, but the plan to go to Palestine fell through, and we were going to go to South America. I don't really know how the decisions of where to go were being made, but finally, a first cousin of my mother's, a renowned man who became the Chief Rabbi of Montreal, Canada – Pinchas Hirschprung – arranged to sponsor us and sent us papers which made our immigration to Canada possible. So in January of 1949, again on my birthday, we landed in Montreal. I was 12 years old at the time and poised for a new life.

I lived in Montreal from 1949 until 1964. My parents worked very hard and built a good life. I finished high school, got a degree in Education and became a teacher. I married Mel and had two wonderful sons, Steve, born in 1959 and Hal in 1964. We moved to the United States in 1964. My father died in Montreal in March 1996. He was two months short of his 94th birthday. He had become a successful businessman there. He was always the optimist who loved his family and was in full possession of his faculties till the very end. My mother was that way too for most of her years and really enjoyed her life, her family and her many activities, the most precious of which were her frequent trips to Israel. Unfortunately she became ill in the late eighties and from then on was never the same person. She was hospitalized in Montreal where, from my home in New York, I visited her at least once a month. She passed away in June 1997.

In 1994 my father arranged for and sponsored Gabi to come to Montreal. She lived in his house for eight months and I saw a lot of her there. I invited her to my home in Stony Brook for a couple of weeks in the summer and showed her Long Island and New York City. We went together to the Holocaust Museum in Washington D.C. We talked and reminisced and she filled me in on many details of our life together during the war. Today, she still lives in that same house in Krakow where for three years, so long ago, I lived too. One of her aunts is still alive, the one who taught me how to read and write. Gabi and I correspond even though I find it hard because my Polish cannot express everything I'd like to say, everything I'd like to ask. She writes me beautiful letters and poems and calls me "little sister". Before my father passed away, he applied for Gabi's mother to be honored by the Yad Vashem in Jerusalem and she was. This is one of mankind's greatest honors and is bestowed on very few. Gabi's mother was deemed to have been deserving of such an honor because by saving my life, she "saved the world entire". Unfortunately she died a short time before she could collect the award herself and so Gabi accepted it in her name which is commemorated on the Mount of Remembrance as one of the Righteous Among Nations, a Memorial which exists today as a testament to those martyrs and heroes who, during humanity's darkest hour, provided a flicker of light.

My father died on March 17, 1996
My mother died on June 14, 1997
My mother's cousin, the rabbi, died in January 1998

Finis

Printed in the United States
144151LV00002B/3/P